MEMOIRS OF DAVID STONER

MEMOIRS OF DAVID STONER

Containing copious extracts from his diary and epistolary correspondence

No man is really happy, rational, virtuous, amiable, but the true Christian. How free from pride is his consciousness of union with the Deity! How free from meanness, the humility which levels him with the worms of the earth! —Craig's Pascal.

EDITED BY
WILLIAM DAWSON & JOHN HANNAH

Shoals, Indiana

Memoirs of David Stoner

Published by Kingsley Press
PO Box 973
Shoals, IN 47581
USA
Tel. (800) 971-7985
www.kingsleypress.com
E-mail: sales@kingsleypress.com

ISBN: 978-1-937428-28-0

First published 1827
First Kingsley Press edition 2012

All rights reserved. No part of this book may be reproduced or transmitted in any form or by any means, electronic or mechanical, including photocopying, recording or by any information storage and retrieval system without written permission from the publisher, except for the inclusion of brief quotations in a review.

Printed in the United States of America.

Contents

Chapter 1: Early Years

Introductory reflections—His birth and parentage—His conversion and its immediate fruits—He goes to an academy at Rochdale—His conduct there—influence of religion in the academy—Importance of early piety...13

Chapter 2: Assistant Teacher

He wishes to obtain a situation—Engages as assistant at Mr. Sigston's academy, Leeds—Arduous nature of his new office—Exemplary manner in which he discharged its duties—He diligently pursues his private studies—Advances in piety—His grateful recollections of the advantages which he enjoyed at Leeds—Affords an instructive example of strict attention to present duty without fruitless anticipations of futurity...23

Chapter 3: Call to the Ministry

Remarks on the Christian ministry—Mr. Stoner's early inclination towards it—His solicitude to ascertain the claims of duty—He carefully examines his views and principles in relation to the ministry—Still hesitates—At length makes two attempts to preach but is discouraged, and desists—Renews his efforts—His observations on a call to the ministry—He is admitted as a probationer on the local preachers' plan, and afterwards placed on the list of reserve—His sentiments on preaching with the Spirit, and on other ministerial qualifications—His diligence in preparing for the pulpit—Anecdote of the Rev. John Smith—He is requested to accompany Dr. Coke to India, but declines—Is recommended to travel, and employed in the Leeds Circuit—His exemplary conduct, and encouraging promise of future eminence..32

Chapter 4: Ministry at Holmfirth

He removes to the Holmfirth Circuit, where he zealously and successfully pursues his ministerial labours—Endangers his health by indiscreet exertion in the pulpit—Observations on this subject—A description of the place of his usual residence—His unabated conviction of the importance of the ministry—Extracts from his letters and diary—Anecdotes of an ignorant hearer, of an infidel, and of a miser—Takes his leave of his friends at Holmfirth and its vicinity with affectionate regret—Remarks on his diligent application to study..50

Chapter 5: Ministry at Huddersfield

He is stationed at Huddersfield—Extracts from his diary—His views of entire sanctification, which he earnestly desires—Still assiduous in his attention to pulpit duty—Part of a letter to Mr. Gilpin—Other extracts from his diary—Record of his diligence in reading and study—He is admitted into full connexion with the Methodist Conference—His marriage—More extracts from his diary—Remarks on his ministerial success and his religious experience during the period he spent at Huddersfield..60

Chapter 6: Ministry at Bradford

Extraordinary success of Mr. Stoner's ministry in the Bradford Circuit, to which he is next appointed—The spirit in which he entered upon his new station—Rev. Isaac Turton's testimony to his zeal and usefulness—Extracts from his diary—He publishes a sermon on occasion of the death of His Majesty, George III—Part of a letter to the Rev. John Hanwell—Other extracts from his diary and correspondence, particularly illustrative of his earnest pursuit of Christian holiness—Remarks on his progress in the attainment of it—Further extracts from his diary and correspondence—Observations on his general habits while at Bradford, and, especially, on his entire conviction of the necessity of divine influence to any degree of ministerial success............74

Chapter 7: Ministry at Birstal

He contemplates a removal to Newcastle-upon-Tyne, but, for special reasons, is appointed to the Birstal Circuit—His unabated zeal and fidelity in that station—He enters upon it with a solemn dedication of himself to God—Extracts from his diary and correspondence—The death of his mother—His diary closes with a satisfactory testimony of his establishment in the Divine life—The fervency of his prayers, whilst at Birstal, for the prosperity of religion—Rules for prayer-meetings—Notice of the domestic afflictions with which he now began to be visited...............125

Chapter 8: Ministry at York

He receives an appointment to the York Circuit—The discussion which took place in Conference on this subject—he has two severe attacks of sickness—Extract from a letter to Miss Milnes—Death of his daughter—Extract from a letter to Mr. William Parkin—Death and character of Mrs. Stoner—Under these painful bereavements, he strives to allay his grief by engaging zealously in the discharge of his official duties—His labours and success—Various extracts from his correspondence—His second marriage—Other extracts—He promotes the erection of a third chapel at York—General remarks on his experience and views during his residence in that city..137

Chapter 9: Last Illness and Death

He unexpectedly receives an appointment to the Liverpool-North Circuit—Closes his ministerial labours at York, and visits two of his former stations on his way to Liverpool—The faithful admonitions which he delivered at Holmfirth—He commences his regular duties at Liverpool with his usual zeal, and with hopeful prospects—His exemplary attention to private devotion—He advances very observably in the Christian life—Extracts from a letter to the Rev. John Slack—Probable occasion of his death—Sketch of his last sermon, with extracts from it—Extracts from a letter to the Rev. Joseph Jennings—The severity of his last illness, his deportment under it, and his truly Christian death—Circumstances of his funeral—Reflections..154

Chapter 10: Character Summary

A description of his character, containing a brief view of his qualities......................................171

Preface

Shortly after the lamented death of Mr. Stoner, several of his friends, who sincerely valued his excellencies and cherished a pleasing though mournful recollection of his labours, expressed a desire that a record of his life, in a separate and distinct form, should be prepared for publication with all convenient speed. Such a record, they imagined, would be highly gratifying to the large circle of his acquaintance, and not wholly unacceptable to others who had heard of him only by report. The compilers of these sheets, whose local situation appeared advantageous for the collection of materials, were requested to arrange the work thus suggested and present it to the public.

To their minds one difficulty occurred. They feared that such a publication would be thought to interfere with the claims of the *Wesleyan-Methodist Magazine*, the vehicle in which, according to the equitable usages of the Connexion, biographical accounts of its departed ministers are generally conveyed. This difficulty, however, was speedily removed by the promptitude and kindness of the Rev. Dr. McAllum, who engaged to furnish a memoir of his esteemed friend for the valuable periodical above mentioned, of as large a size as its pages, occupied as they are with other important matter, could conveniently admit. Dr. McAllum's very elegant and interesting sketch appeared in the *Magazine* for May, 1827. By his permission, granted with his usual frankness and urbanity, the compilers have gratefully availed themselves of its contents, particularly in narrating Mr. Stoner's proceedings while at York and in describing the virtues which adorned his exemplary character. To offer their public thanks to the Doctor is now, alas! too late. He also has finished his earthly course in the prime of his days, leaving in the hearts of all who knew him a deep and tender regret that one so amiable, gifted, and promising should be withdrawn so soon from the circle of his social intercourse and ministerial exertions.

From Mr. Stoner's manuscripts the compilers proceeded to make such a selection as they deemed most suitable to their purpose, and also applied to many of his friends in different parts of the country for facts, letters, or other communications. They soon found themselves placed under very agreeable obligations, for their applications were immediately met with a cheerfulness and confidence which they beg most affectionately to acknowledge. The names of their esteemed correspondents—with one or two exceptions where secrecy was desired—will appear in connexion with their contributions; and if this work be at all calculated to accomplish the important objects for which it is prepared, it will undoubtedly prove a source of much satisfaction to those who have thus promoted its compilation, that to their kind attention and assistance no small part of its worth is justly attributable.

Ample materials were quickly obtained, but it seemed at first rather difficult to fix upon such a plan as would bring them into the most profitable use. They were not sufficient to form a regular piece or biography, unaccompanied by observations; and they were too valuable to be merged in a continued narration without any distinct reference or lengthened citation. To the compilers it appeared most advisable to divide the whole work into chapters corresponding to the leading periods of Mr. Stoner's life, with the reserve of one chapter in conclusion for a delineation of his character; to arrange the different facts and extracts with as much attention to chronological accuracy as was practicable or necessary; and to enrich each chapter with as many extracts as their collections afforded without descending to tedious minuteness or indulging in needless repetitions. They have used much diligence to secure correctness even in matters seemingly trivial, for they think that the very circumstances of sacred truth demand attention; and they have interspersed such reflections as were suggested by the successive events which they record. These may in themselves be sufficiently obvious and common, but it is hoped that they will derive some interest and force from the bright example with which they are associated.

Not a few of Mr. Stoner's connexions and general acquaintance have urged the propriety of appending specimens of his sermons to the memoirs. This the compilers once intended, but they were restrained chiefly by two considerations: first, that the addition of such specimens would greatly increase the size of the volume, extended perhaps already beyond its just limits; and secondly, that some purpose is entertained, if circumstances encourage it, of publishing a selection of the sermons in a separate form. From a cursory examination of Mr. Stoner's discourses, the compilers do not hesitate to pronounce that, notwithstanding the multitude of pulpit compositions which are continually issuing front the press, such a volume, if edited with judgment and care, would prove a valuable accession to the religious productions of the day. In the ninth chapter of this work is inserted a sketch of Mr. Stoner's last sermon, with a few extracts from its more striking passages. The compilers once purposed to introduce other sketches in different parts of the memoirs on the same plan but were apprehensive that these would too far interrupt the progress of the narration and in some degree change the biographical character of the work. Enough, it is presumed, will be found scattered through the successive chapters and contained in the outline mentioned above to convey a correct idea of Mr. Stoner's talent and style of preaching. More than this did not seem to fall properly within the province of his biographers.

It is an encouraging circumstance to the compilers that so much solicitude has been expressed for the speedy publication of these memoirs, but they fear that they have incurred censure by seeming delay. They beg to allege, in their own excuse, that they have done what they could to expedite the work. Nine months have not yet elapsed since the death of Mr. Stoner, a period which they trust will not be deemed immoderately long when it is considered that they have enjoyed no peculiar facilities for despatch. They wish to state farther that, as they had to draw their materials from a large and mingled mass of private correspondence, and from the manuscripts of Mr. Stoner, all of which are written in a very small character and continually interspersed with short-hand, it was necessary that every line should be carefully transcribed for the press. They may also be allowed to mention that their task has been pursued amid the constant pressure of other engagements, the frequent languors of personal indisposition, and repeated visitations of domestic suffering and bereavement. Oftener than once has he on whom, from his situation, the more laborious part of this compilation necessarily devolved, attempted to prosecute his work with a trembling hand and aching heart while a beloved child lay in the adjoining room wrapped in the pale vestments of mortality. He enters not into affecting particulars. Private griefs are of too delicate and retiring a nature to be obtruded without necessity on public notice. These are introduced merely to account, in part, for apparent inattention to the solicitations of friendship; and they shall now repose for ever in their own sanctuary—the perpetual but silent recollections of parental feeling.

The work is at length committed to public view with unaffected diffidence. Had the compilers been favoured with more undisturbed leisure, or a longer space of time, they might have rendered it more accurate and less unworthy of the exemplary man whose history it reviews. Small and hasty, however, as their offering is, they humbly consecrate it to him from whom all truth and virtue emanate, praying that he may prosper it to the advancement of his praise. If it be deemed utterly unfit to accomplish anything truly beneficial, they will resign it quietly to that gulf of oblivion which has already received many other compositions undertaken from motives equally pure and executed with ability far superior.

One thing more it may not be unnecessary to mention—that the compilers have not the slightest pecuniary interest in the publication. The profits are entirely appropriated to the use of Mr. Stoner's family. A gentleman of Leeds has kindly engaged to superintend all that relates to this point; and from what the compilers know of his character, they are fully assured that he will conduct the whole with the utmost attention and care, and apply the proceeds with fidelity and discretion.

WILLIAM DAWSON
JOHN HANNAH
Leeds, July 16th, 1827

Advertisement to the Second Edition

In this edition the compilers have endeavoured to correct the errors which had escaped their attention in passing the former one through the press; but they have refrained from changing the character of the work by unnecessary alterations or unimportant additions. The copyright is now sold to the committee appointed to manage the affairs of the Methodist Book Room, and the sum procured for it will be applied to the use of Mr. Stoner's family.

W. D.
J. H.
Manchester, June 11th, 1829

Note to the Kingsley Press Edition

The Kingsley Press edition of this work has been prepared from the tenth edition, published by the Wesleyan Conference Office, City Road, London.

This edition is completely unabridged. British spelling and usage have been retained throughout. Some very minimal modernizing of punctuation has taken place—mostly the removal of unneccesary commas for the benefit of modern readers.

1

Early Years

Introductory reflections—His birth and parentage—His conversion and its immediate fruits—He goes to an academy at Rochdale—His conduct there—influence of religion in the academy—Importance of early piety.

THE early death of persons eminent for their piety, talents, and useful services in the Christian church awakens serious and melancholy reflection. It is one of the inscrutable mysteries of divine providence. Men prepare instruments for use and employ them in the execution of their proper offices; God often prepares instruments, places them in situations of hopeful and promising labour and, while we admire their qualifications and gratefully anticipate rich results from their activity and zeal, snatches them suddenly from our eyes and declares the supremacy of his control and the independence of his will. To inquire why he acts thus is natural but unwise.

"Clouds and darkness" surround the throne of the Most High. Mortal conjecture cannot penetrate the thick and awful veil. Eternity alone will draw it aside and reveal its hidden wonders. Reason is taught to sit in silence at God's feet. "Behold, he taketh away: who can hinder him? Who," presuming to interfere with his counsels, or attempting to restrain his hand, "will say unto him, What doest thou?" The language of meek and adoring submission is the proper language of man. "The Lord gave, and the Lord hath taken away; blessed be the name of the Lord."

Such events, however, demand attention. They are full of instruction. They loudly proclaim the frailty of human nature even in its best estate and testify that man is indeed a bubble, floating awhile on the wave which gave him birth, then bursting and sinking into the common mass. They admonish survivers to cultivate a spirit of vigilance, promptitude, and despatch—to "work while it is day" because "the night cometh, when no man can work." They attract our notice to the religious character of those who thus pass prematurely and unexpectedly away and give a more affecting and powerful energy to their holy example. To present that example to public view is at once a tribute of friendship and a discharge of duty. Shall the departure of such men be "folded up in silence?" Shall it be deemed enough to shed our unavailing regrets over their graves, while we suppress their monitory principles, actions, and precepts? No. Though dead, they yet speak—and speak in accents deepened and strengthened by the solemnities of the tomb which has opened its mouth to receive them. Everything invites us to review their progress through life, to examine their Christian tempers, to mark their high and majestic aims, and to weigh their salutary counsels. "Remember them who have spoken unto you the Word of God: whose faith follow, considering the end of their conversation," and reposing in the assurance that "Jesus Christ," the refuge of the sinner and the joy of the saint, unchanged by the lapse of time and the various fluctuations of this earthly scene, is "the same yesterday, and today, and for ever."

Reflections like these are suggested by the removal of him who forms the subject of these memoirs. He is snatched away in the forenoon of life, when his friends were fondly expecting a lengthened day of valuable services. He had just entered upon a new field of labour—a field of large extent, importance, and promise; but scarcely had he commenced his work when he passed into his rest. He is gone. "The eye that had seen him shall see him no more." Tender recollections arise. The tear of friendship mingles with the sorrows of domestic bereavement and mourns the death of one of the "excellent of the earth." But other duties call and engage us to "gather up the fragments that remain" of his Christian experience and holy actions "that nothing be lost." To his connexions and acquaintance generally, and especially to his younger brethren in the ministry, it is hoped that it will not be uninteresting or unprofitable to exhibit the "grace of God in him."

Happy, if any catch his falling mantle, imbibe his spirit, and imitate his conduct. Then, he will neither have lived nor died in vain.

David Stoner was born at Barwick-in-Elmet, a village about seven miles from Leeds, on Sunday, April 6th, 1794. The retired situation of his native place was friendly to the constitutional timidity of his mind, and its religious privileges afforded him peculiar assistances. His parents were decidedly pious; and, sensible of the inestimable value of an immortal spirit, they laboured to restrain him from all evil and teach him the "way of righteousness." Religion was presented to his consideration under the most pleasing aspect, explained in affectionate precept, and recommended by daily example. His father still survives to lament this bright "coal" which is "quenched" in Israel. His mother, who, for maternal solicitude, may justly be classed with Hannah the mother of Samuel, Eunice the mother of Timothy, and Monica the mother of Augustine, has exchanged mortality for life. Her end was peace. The tender assiduities of his parents were not fruitless. They scattered the seeds of truth and piety in his heart, which, watered by the dews and showers of divine influence, yielded a rich and blessed harvest. They collected material around the hallowing altar on which they desired to offer the services of their child to God; and when the fire descended from heaven and the breath of divine inspiration fanned its kindling ardours, the sacrifice arose in flames of heavenly desire and humble love. Their success furnishes another practical evidence of the vast utility of pious parental exertion. To such exertion God himself has given the strongest commendation: "Shall I hide from Abraham that thing which I do? For I know him, that he will command his children and his household after him, and they shall keep the way of the Lord, to do justice and judgment; that the Lord may bring upon Abraham that which he hath spoken of him."

It would not have appeared extraordinary if one trained from his infancy to the knowledge of religion had been conducted by a more gradual method to the fuller apprehension and enjoyment of its truth. His conversion, however, was very clearly and strongly marked. In the year 1806 Barwick and its neighbourhood were visited with a severe affliction of an inflammatory nature which swept many into eternity and excited considerable alarm. Among others who died was the pious father of a large family. One of the writers of these pages was desired to preach on the occasion, which he did on the morning of Good Friday, from Deut. 32:29: "O that they were wise, that they understood this, that they would consider their latter end!" While the preacher was endeavouring to urge the admonitions suggested by his text on the consciences of his hearers, young Stoner, whose mind had been much affected by the instances of mortality which had taken place around him, felt the word in demonstration and power. He distinctly saw that if his heart and life were not changed "his latter end" would be death. During that day he laboured under a painful conviction of his sin and misery, and at a prayer-meeting held in the chapel the same evening could no longer suppress his feelings. He cried aloud for mercy, sought the favour of God with his whole heart, found it, and went home rejoicing. To that day he always adverted with peculiar pleasure. On the first page of his diary, which he did not begin to keep until many years afterwards, he briefly and emphatically writes, "Awakened and converted, April 4th, Good Friday, 1806." To persons who have observed the rapid formation of habits, especially in early youth, it will not appear improbable that the benefit which he received at a meeting for prayer tended to strengthen his attachment in subsequent life to similar assemblies. He never indeed allowed them to supersede other ordinances, but regarded them as valuable auxiliaries to all, engaging the united faith, and hope, and fervour of Christians, and often securing the special presence and blessing of God.

His friends rejoiced over the important change which had been wrought in his views, temper, and conduct; but considering his age, only just twelve years, they rejoiced with trembling. They feared that when the passions of youth grew into vigour and maturity, when the charms of an untried world presented their fascinations and allurements, and when temptation assailed him in its innumerable forms, he, like many others, might "be led away with the error of the wicked, and fall from his own steadfastness." To prevent this, they watched over him with jealousy and care. Happily, their fears were not realized.

He began, continued, and ended well. The foundation was laid deep, and the building rose rapidly and regularly, firm in its structure and lovely in its appearance, till the "head-stone thereof" was "brought forth with shoutings, Grace, grace unto it."

From the time of his conversion he was remarkably serious, thoughtful, and observant. He possessed the desirable talent of applying everything to a practical use and deriving instruction from any valuable hint, whether addressed to himself or to others. One example of this has been preserved in the memory of a friend. A person who met in the same class was complaining to his leader that he felt himself greatly discouraged by various temptations and particularly by Satan's suggesting to his mind that he had no religion. "Well, brother," said the leader, "I would advise you to take advantage of the devil and say to him, 'If I have no religion, by the grace of God I will never rest until I obtain it;' and by this means, whether you have or have not religion, the temptation will be overruled for your good." This remark struck Stoner's mind very forcibly. He mentioned it repeatedly afterwards and, in seasons of depression and discouragement, endeavoured to act consistently with it. To be *right* was his great aim; and if a suspicion arose that perhaps, after all, he was the dupe of self-delusion, he did not suffer himself to sink into a state of inactivity and despair, but renewed his exercises of self-examination, prayer, and diligence.

At this early period he was commendably solicitous for the spiritual happiness of others and gave some promise of the important office which he ultimately sustained in the church of Christ. Shortly after he was brought to the saving enjoyment of religion, a very gracious influence was felt among the young people of his native village. He laboured assiduously to promote it, and often met with his juvenile associates in fields, barns, and other places for the purposes of prayer and mutual exhortation. He was styled their *preacher*; and even then was remarkable for the clearness, pungency, and force of his addresses. Those days he always regarded as eminently happy. Several of his early friends have not yet forgotten the zealous and affecting admonitions which they at that time received from him. Meetings of young persons like those mentioned ought undoubtedly to be encouraged with much caution. They are liable to abuse, and may unawares engender levity and pride. In this instance, however, they appear to have produced good effects only. David Stoner was discreet beyond his years and, under the direction of older advisers, was careful to "abstain from all appearance of evil."

The time had now arrived when his parents began to think of preparing him for a suitable station in future life. This occasioned them some perplexity. His abstraction of mind, his strong propensity to studious pursuits, and his inaptitude for the ordinary avocations of business seemed to militate against his being fixed in such a situation as they had at first intended for him. They sought direction, however, from the God of providence; and at length, after much deliberation, resolved to follow the suggestion of a friend and train him for a literary or mercantile employment. With this design, in the beginning of the year 1808, he was placed under the care of Mr. Bridge, who at that time kept an academy at Rochdale.

Temptations attend every change in life, and those to which serious young persons are subjected by a removal to school are often perilous. New scenes are opened, new connexions are formed, new engagements arise; and not unfrequently the tender plant of juvenile piety, placed in a fresh and perhaps unfriendly soil, exposed to furious storms and withering blights, and deprived of the fostering hand of religious care and attention, decays and dies. Providentially, this was not the case with David Stoner. The school to which he was sent proved a nursery of piety as well as of learning. Here he extended his religious acquaintance and enjoyed peculiar advantages; here he not only preserved his spiritual attainments but continued to "grow in grace and in the knowledge of our Lord and Saviour Jesus Christ."

While he was at Rochdale, he had among his associates William Lord and Samuel Wilde, both now honourably and usefully employed in the Wesleyan ministry. They unite in their testimony to the excellency of his character and consistency of his deportment. Mr. Lord, whose acquaintance with him was long and intimate, has kindly furnished the writers of these memoirs with some interesting and valuable communications. "I well remember," says Mr. L., "that when he came to the school his appearance was rather forbidding, owing to his being tall and rustic in his manners and dress. But his progress in learning soon convinced his tutors that he possessed a mind of a superior order; while his mild and peaceable conduct secured him the good opinion of all and the friendship of many of his schoolfellows. He was remarkable for a diligent application to his studies and an indifference to the games and sports of which schoolboys in general are so fond. At that time taciturnity and modesty were as conspicuous traits of his character as in any subsequent part of his life."

"During the time," adds Mr. L., "that we were schoolfellows, there was a blessed work of God upon the minds of many of the boys. Several met in class and I have no doubt enjoyed the power and comforts of religion, of which number David Stoner was one. Mr. Bridge favoured us with a room in which, at proper seasons, we held prayer-meetings. On some of these occasions great numbers of the boys attended, and David Stoner and others engaged in prayer, frequently with peculiar propriety, fluency, and fervour; and not seldom the power of God was present to wound and to heal."

At Rochdale he also formed an acquaintance, which ripened into a very sincere friendship, with the late Mr. Gregory, of Nottingham. Mr. G. was at the same academy and was one of the serious and devout boys mentioned above. Several letters afterwards passed between him and D. Stoner. By the kindness of Mr. Shelton, brother-in-law of Mr. G., the writers are favoured with all the letters of Mr. Stoner that could be found and with which some of the succeeding pages will be enriched. They are much worn and were, doubtless, often read by the lamented friend to whom they are addressed. These two were affecting victims of mortality. They pursued different paths through life but happily maintained the same religious principles and aims. They were associated in early friendship and early death and have undoubtedly rejoined each other in the "quiet shades of paradise." Their intimacy on earth was the source of mutual gratification. "I often think," says Mr. Stoner in one of his letters, "what a blessing it was that ever we met at Rochdale. What refreshing seasons did we use to have from the presence of the Lord!" His Nottingham friend was never known to mention him without lively satisfaction and pleasure.

Mr. Gregory quitted the academy first. To him D. Stoner writes, September 4th, 1808, and informs him of an accident which had befallen him and interrupted some of his engagements—the breaking of his arm. He expresses an earnest trust that his friend was still directing his face toward the heavenly Zion, "fighting against the world, the flesh, and the devil;" and adds that, "for his own part, he was determined to proceed in the narrow way." "I hope," says he, with affectionate emphasis, "that I have an interest in your prayers as you have in mine." He mentions the departure of several of the boys from school and the need he felt of Mr. G.'s assistance. He discovers also some solicitude in relation to his future movements, but subjoins, "There is a promise which says, 'Seek ye first the kingdom of God, and his righteousness; and all other things shall be added unto you.'"

In a letter to the same friend, dated November 3rd, 1808, he says, "For myself, though I have been a trifler and am yet very unfaithful, I feel determined, through God's grace, to serve him with all my heart, to give myself up into his hands and let him work as 'seemeth him good.' I am cheered with the hope that we have only a few more fleeting years at farthest to weather out, to take up our cross, deny ourselves, and live happily below; and shall then receive an eternity, a heaven of happiness above. O dear Robert, pray, pray for me; for 'the effectual prayer of a righteous man availeth much.'" Such an extract demands no remark: it sufficiently attests the serious and devotional temper of the writer's mind.

At this time it appears that there was an uncommon religious influence in the academy. "We have had a great increase of late," adds Mr. S. in the same letter. "The Lord has been shaking the dry bones, so that upwards of a dozen boys attend the class-meetings." Part of this letter is written by a mutual friend, Mr. John Crawshaw, who observes, "Surely God dwells among us and hath chosen this house for his own. When *you* were here we had good meetings, but those which are now held among us far surpass them. A number of little boys will collect together and tell of God's goodness to them with all the simplicity of little children. Indeed, they can scarcely be called anything else; but, young as they are, God has dealt bountifully with them and made them very happy. Scarcely a week passes but one youth or more is made happy. O that you were here to join us! God bless you. I don't know that there is a boy in the school who does not sometimes attend the prayer-meetings."

It is justly lamented that religious impressions on companies of young people, particularly at schools, are often transient. Some leave; others come. Some perhaps prove extravagant, others unfaithful. An attentive observer of human life will not be surprised to discover that this was partially the case at Rochdale. In May, 1809, Mr. Stoner writes to the same correspondent, "We are rather dead in religion at the school. There are only four or five, besides the masters, who attend the class-meetings." Such changes occur, but they do not prove that preceding visitations of heavenly influence were either imaginary or useless. They forcibly indeed declare the necessity of caution, fidelity, and diligence, but ought by no means to impeach the condescension and mercy of God. If the "morning cloud" seems to vanish from the sky, and the "early dew" from the earth, let it not be denied that they have been there or supposed that their effects have, in every instance, utterly perished.

Whatever might be the state of others, David Stoner continued to urge on his Christian course. He complains, indeed, in the letter last mentioned, that he had not been sufficiently watchful nor made such progress in the ways of religion as he ought to have made, but expresses his hope that God would "quicken his soul and make him a good Christian." A revival of religion had just taken place at Nottingham, on which he remarks, with his characteristic energy, "I am very glad to hear that the Lord is prospering his work at Nottingham; and I hope he will carry it on until the wicked man cannot find a wicked companion in the whole town."

The time which he spent at Rochdale was a year and a half. He took his leave of his friends there at Midsummer of 1809 and immediately afterwards engaged in that situation which will form the subject of the following chapter.

From the brief portion of his life which has already been reviewed there arises a powerful argument in favour of the importance of early piety. It was this which preserved David Stoner from the evils to which boyhood is liable and gave a direction to his views, purposes, and actions, honourable to his God, happy for himself, and beneficial to others. Let every young person who reads these memoirs copy his example. "Youth is not rich in time;" let that time be diligently employed. Youth is the spring season of life's short year, when the seeds of the future harvest ought to be plentifully sown; it is the morning of life's short day, the mild and sacred hours of which ought to be carefully spent. Who dares calculate on lengthened life? or, if life be lengthened, what is of greater moment than to consecrate it from its commencement to God and heaven? With regard to many, much time has already elapsed. "Remember," says a distinguished Roman Emperor, "how long thou last deferred thy most important concern, and how often thou hast neglected the opportunities afforded thee. It is time for thee at length to consider thy situation in this world, of which thou art a part; and what the wise Governor of the world, from whom thou art derived, requires of thee. Thou hast a circumscribed space of time assigned thee, which if thou dost not employ in making all calm and serene within, it will pass away, and thou wilt pass away, and it will not return." (Marcus Antoninus, lib. ii., cap. 4.)

2

Assistant Teacher

He wishes to obtain a situation—Engages as assistant at Mr. Sigston's academy, Leeds—Arduous nature of his new office—Exemplary manner in which he discharged its duties—He diligently pursues his private studies—Advances in piety—His grateful recollections of the advantages which he enjoyed at Leeds—Affords an instructive example of strict attention to present duty without fruitless anticipations of futurity.

IT was young Stoner's object to procure a situation as soon as possible in which he might combine opportunities of personal improvement with useful service and release his parents from the charges of his education. When he had been a year at Rochdale, he ventured to apply for the office of under-assistant in a school at Leeds, but was not thought sufficiently grounded in the elements of Latin to perform the duties that would be expected from him. He continued awhile in suspense. Mr. Bridge signified a wish to employ him in his academy, but his proposals do not appear to have been satisfactory. He returned, therefore, as a scholar to Rochdale, hoping that in the course of another half-year some situation might present itself to which his abilities and attainments would be deemed adequate.

At this season of comparative perplexity he did not fail to commit himself, by prayer and resignation, to the guidance of divine providence. He "acknowledged" God and God "directed his paths." He purposed to offer himself as a bookkeeper or writer in any other department and requested his friend Mr. Gregory, if he heard of any such situation, to inform him of it. But on his quitting Rochdale, he succeeded in obtaining what was far more suited to his views and dispositions, the place of assistant in Mr. Sigston's academy, Leeds. Here he enjoyed every advantage that he could reasonably expect or desire; and here he remained until he was called into the regular work of the ministry. It was no inconsiderable addition to his comfort that, during a part of this time, his old schoolfellow and friend, Mr. Lord, was associated with him as assistant in the same seminary.

The office which a teacher of youth sustains is arduous and perplexing. To ascertain the peculiar temper and talent of each scholar; to restrain the confident, encourage the diffident, and quicken the slothful; to convey instruction in the clearest, most engaging, and most effectual manner; to attend properly to the formation of principles and character, by far the most important object of education; and to maintain a sufficient degree of self-government and control is confessed by those who are most experienced in the work of tuition to be no easy task. To young persons like David Stoner it must be very trying. He was, however, under the constant direction of his seniors; his early habits were friendly to his new engagements; and in the honourable but difficult office of teaching youth he was by degrees more fully trained for the station which he afterwards occupied.

Of the laudable manner in which he discharged the duties of this situation, the most satisfactory testimonies are given. "His conduct in my house," says Mr. Sigston, "was most exemplary. His qualifications for teaching were peculiarly good. His manner was prompt but firm, and he communicated instruction with pleasantness mingled with gravity. He felt much for the salvation of the young persons under his care; and in several instances, I doubt not, his pious endeavours for their spiritual good were crowned with success." The testimony of Mr. Lord, with whom he lived on terms of the most friendly intimacy, is very similar. To these may be added the evidence of Mr. William Gilpin, who was a scholar in Mr. Sigston's academy during part of the time that Mr. Stoner was engaged as an assistant, and who gratefully acknowledges that he owes much to the influence of Mr. Stoner's example and admonitory communications.

"Though then but young," says Mr. G., "I no sooner became an inmate in Mr. Sigston's establishment than I was forcibly struck with the character and deportment of my venerated friend. Habitually grave and serious, his very appearance served to repress levity and excite respect. On persons who enjoyed no intimacy with him, his extreme natural reserve was apt to produce an unfavourable impression; but such an impression was instantly removed by a more familiar acquaintance. He was eminently affectionate, and when he unbosomed himself on any subject there was a peculiar charm in his conversation, tone, and manner. He was accustomed to embrace every seasonable opportunity of addressing the scholars respecting their salvation; and the effects of his instructions, counsels, and admonitions are found in several individuals at the present day. It is almost unnecessary to add that the boys in general were remarkably attached to him."

While he approved himself thus faithful in executing the duties of his office, he was also very attentive to his personal improvement. The time which he was expected to spend in the business of teaching was six hours each day; he consequently had many intervals which he did not neglect to occupy in his private studies. "From the time of his coming to me," adds Mr. Sigston, "he discovered an ardent thirst after knowledge; and being of a studious and reserved disposition employed most of his leisure time in the acquisition of various parts of literature, the knowledge of which his situation and prospects seemed to require."

"His thirst for knowledge," observes Mr. Gilpin, "was insatiable. He was, therefore, extremely diligent in the improvement of every leisure moment. Whoever trifled, he was sure to be busy. Indeed, his industry at that period, then about seventeen years of age, was the most striking feature in his character; nor is there any reason to think that he ever relaxed his efforts to advance in knowledge as well as in piety. No man ever reminded me so forcibly of a racer in the Grecian games as my late friend; he was always at full speed."

One part of his attention was very properly directed to the attainment of languages; and he appears, while at Mr. Sigston's, to have made considerable progress in the Greek and Latin, French and Portuguese tongues. To these he afterwards added so much knowledge of the Hebrew as enabled him to examine the original text of the Old Testament with some degree of facility, and to guard his expositions of that portion of holy writ against the loose conjectures of fanciful etymology and the illusions of a visionary philosophy. Mr. Sigston had in his family a Portuguese and a Spaniard; Stoner therefore possessed peculiar helps for the study of those languages, of which, in regard to the Portuguese, he eagerly availed himself, and that with speedy and singular success. It cannot be supposed that, amidst the multiplicity of his avocations, his classical acquirements were of the very first order. They seem to have been useful rather than eminent; and they were sacredly devoted to those higher objects which he habitually contemplated.

To subjects of general information also, and particularly to select theological publications, he applied much of his time. He is said to have been a remarkably rapid reader. He certainly was a very attentive one. What is related of the excellent Scougal, a man resembling himself in richness of promise and brevity of life, may, without impropriety, be applied to him: "He did not so much *read* books as *think* them."[1] In his epistolary correspondence are inserted several short notices of the works which passed under his examination—notices strongly marked by sagacity, discrimination, and intelligence. Sometimes he made extracts from the books he read, and generally availed himself of such other methods as were most agreeable to the habits of his own mind, and best adapted to bring the contents of his reading into profitable use, as well as to preserve them in his memory.

Amidst the various and multiplied engagements of a teacher and student there is no little danger of spiritual declension. Religion may not be forgotten; its profession may not be relinquished; but its truths may fail to exert their wonted influence, and its enjoyments may languish. It is exceedingly possible for the mind to employ itself in the acquisition of speculative knowledge while the heart unawares declines in heavenly love. From this evil Mr. Stoner seems generally to have been preserved. The situation in which he was placed afforded him peculiar helps of a religious nature. At Mr. Sigston's he found a nursery where his Christian virtues were protected and invigorated, and where the tender blossoms of divine grace, opening in his experience and practice, were saved from the insidious worm of evil principles and the pernicious frost of sinful company. He also enjoyed the advantages of a zealous and efficient ministry, and appears to have derived much assistance from the sermons which he then heard, outlines of many of which have been discovered among

---

1   See Wesley's Christian Library, vol. xxiii., p. 251. 8vo. edit.

his papers. He was likewise particularly attentive to the holy Scriptures, which he made his daily study. In one of his letters to Mr. Gregory, he emphatically styles the Bible, "The book of books, the book of God, and the god of books;" and, after quoting the eloquent testimonies of Sir William Jones in proof of its excellency, observes, "I well remember a remark which I have somewhere heard or read: 'God follows you out of your bed-chamber with a jealous eye in a morning to see what book lies nearest your heart; whether the first book you open be *his* or one on some trivial subject.' This observation I generally recollect, and consequently read God's book the first, which is a kind of divine antidote against all the poisonous qualities of others." But the religious state of his mind at this period will be best illustrated by a few extracts from his free and confidential correspondence.

To Mr. Gregory he writes, August 9th, 1809, shortly after he entered upon his new situation: "As for my *better part,* I trust I am advancing faster in the way to heaven than ever I did. The Lord often blesses my soul in a powerful manner. O what a good God have we to do with! After all the sins we have committed against him, after all our backslidings from him, he has mercy on us still. Dear Sir, let us press forward to the mark for the prize of our high calling in Christ Jesus."

On January 11th, 1810, he writes to the same correspondent from Barwick: "I am very glad to hear you have made so great advancement in the paths of religion, but am sorry to find that you have been so much afflicted. What a blessing it is, however, to have the fear of death taken away! If God had taken you to himself, to paradise, to eternal glory, before me, O I think how you would have welcomed me when the Lord had pleased to call me to the regions of everlasting day. O ravishing thought! O boundless love! O infinite mercy! I hope you remember the words of the blessed apostle when he says, 'Our light affliction, which is but for a moment, worketh for us a far more exceeding and eternal weight of glory.' The more patiently we suffer, the greater will be our reward. For my own part, I know not where to begin to praise the Lord. When I consider into what a situation I have got, contrary to all expectation; when I reflect how many young men, after leaving school, have waited several years before they could obtain a place in which they might earn their bread, whilst no sooner did I return home than this was handed out by providence, a situation so desirable, so advantageous in every point of view, particularly for the better part; when I attend to these things, I feel that I can with propriety adopt the heart-cheering words of the poet and say,

> When all thy mercies, O my God!
> My rising soul surveys,
> Transported with the view, I'm lost
> In wonder, love, and praise.

"If ever I lived in happiness, I do now. Being at a covenant-meeting this new year, I was so enabled to deliver up my soul to God by living faith as I never was before. I had been reading in the *Methodist Magazine* for January and February, 1799, a sermon concerning the scriptural *method of believing in order to obtain present and eternal salvation,* from John 6:29: 'This is the work of God, that ye believe on him whom he hath sent.' I think I never heard or read the way of faith so plainly described. The author says that 'believing in order to obtain salvation is a lifting up of the heart to Christ in earnest desire, the receiving of him with fervent affections, the conversing daily and hourly with him in supplication and praise, the looking to him with a single eye and diligently hearkening to his voice.' I have likewise thought very much of late on the word *eternity,* which may be found in Isa. 57:15. This has been a spur to my soul; but still I feel to my hurt the old corruptions of my nature arise and trouble me. I hope the constant cry of my heart is, 'Lord, I am thine: save me from pride, anger, and all other things that are contrary to thy will!' Please to recollect," he adds in a postscript, "that *tempus fugit;* and also remember to pray, pray, pray, pray for me!"

In a letter to the same excellent friend, dated June 9th, 1810, he gratefully mentions the happiness he enjoyed in the society of Mr. Lord, who had at that time begun to preach. "He truly lightens all my burdens by taking a large share of them. We can open our minds to each other; reprove, admonish, encourage, edify, strengthen, and bear with each other, and thus 'fulfil the law of Christ.' I feel my soul at full stretch," he observes, "for all the mind that was in Christ. The Lord grant it to us for Christ's sake!" In the postscript of this letter he adds, in larger character, doubtless as an expression of his own desires and a direction to his correspondent, the Vulgate translation of that comprehensive beatitude, Matt. 5:6, "Blessed are they which do hunger and thirst after righteousness: for they shall be filled"— "quoniam ipsi *saturabuntur.*"[1]

September 22nd, 1810, he writes to the same: "I am glad to hear you wish to be more like your divine head. I could wish the same. I want a *steady, firm fixedness to the point,* and that is to glorify God in everything. O sir, if you and I, in every circumstance of life, could only do the same that Christ would have done had he been in it, how delightfully we should go on! Heaven on the road to heaven. Brother Lord seems to me to be devoted to the service of God. He is very lively; and, thank God, we live together in peace and unity. I trust that we both have communion with the Holy Spirit. O may I, you, and he be continually leaving the 'things that are behind' and stretching forward, through sunshine and darkness, to the 'prize of our high calling,' that is, a heart emptied of pride and 'filled with all the fulness of God.' I feel the temptations of youth very strong. May the Lord assist me to overcome them! I want my heart sanctifying from all its pollutions, making holy, and entirely devoted to God. Pray for me! If you have any interest at the throne of grace, O make use of it for me!"

During the former part of the time that he spent at Mr. Sigston's, he experienced much bodily languor and debility, he grew very fast, and occasionally discovered symptoms of an unfavourable nature in reference to his health. In the spring of 1810, he was so feeble that sometimes he could scarcely walk, nay, very often fell down. By the kind attentions of Mrs. Sigston, however, and his own regular habits, accompanied with the blessing of God, he soon acquired strength; and, as he advanced towards maturity, became more capable of active and vigorous exertion, though his constitution seems never to have been a firm one.

---

1   Italicization in original.

To the advantages which he possessed in the seminary at Leeds, he always referred with grateful and affectionate feeling. Writing to the Rev. John Smith, whose society he enjoyed for a season as a Christian friend and assistant in the same establishment, he styles Claypit Academy, "that lovely, delightfully remembered spot." And in a letter addressed to Mr. Sigston from Holmfirth he gives utterance to his recollections in the following terms: "As soon as I think of writing to you, what a number of ideas, what a diversity of emotions, rush into my mind and fill my trembling soul! Gratitude and humiliation, joy and grief, pleasure and pain, by turns transport and depress my agitated heart. No sooner does your name present itself to my recollection than I am involuntarily led to take a retrospect of my life for the past six years. The former and greater part of that period I spent under your hospitable roof and watchful eye. You cared for my welfare. You promoted my increase of knowledge. You bore with my youthful levities, with my crooked natural dispositions, with my careless inconsiderateness, my wanderings from duty, my derelictions of principle; and under your superintending care the youth approached to manhood. Surely then I ought to evince my gratitude by every possible token of dutiful affection, and such a token I humbly hope you will consider the lines you are now reading."

To a person who attentively surveys Mr. Stoner's conduct in the youthful part of his life, one thing must appear particularly deserving of regard: that he was always careful to discharge the duties which lay before him with diligence and assiduity and without indulging vain anticipations of futurity. Many neglect this. They direct their minds to the uncertain occurrences of subsequent life; the period will arrive, they fondly imagine, when they shall have an object correspondent to their powers; in the meantime, the duties of their present station are either entirely neglected or carelessly performed. Such ruin their own projects. The precious season in which they ought to lay the foundation of future eminence and usefulness is wasted; and the irresolution, indolence, and propensity to indulge in visionary schemes, which mark the proceedings of their early days, usually attend them through life. To persons of this description David Stoner stands in pointed and instructive contrast. Resigning the contingencies of futurity to the direction of providence, he was solicitous to perform the duty of the day in its day. "He who is faithful in that which is little" affords the best hope that he will be "faithful also in much." Fidelity in one situation prepares for honourable employment in another. This was exemplified in the subject of these memoirs. He was faithful in teaching the boys the rudiments of learning, and was gradually fitted for the high office of teaching men the truths and blessings of religion. The steps by which he was conducted into this wider and more important sphere of beneficial labour will next demand our attention.

3

Call to the Ministry

Remarks on the Christian ministry—Mr. Stoner's early inclination towards it—His solicitude to ascertain the claims of duty—He carefully examines his views and principles in relation to the ministry—Still hesitates—At length makes two attempts to preach but is discouraged, and desists—Renews his efforts—His observations on a call to the ministry—He is admitted as a probationer on the local preachers' plan, and afterwards placed on the list of reserve—His sentiments on preaching with the Spirit, and on other ministerial qualifications—His diligence in preparing for the pulpit—Anecdote of the Rev. John Smith—He is requested to accompany Dr. Coke to India, but declines—Is recommended to travel, and employed in the Leeds Circuit—His exemplary conduct, and encouraging promise of future eminence.

He who undertakes the office of the Christian ministry engages in a work beyond all others important and difficult. The truths which his duty requires him to inculcate are divine and heavenly, embracing the highest interests of the soul and connecting themselves with the destinies of eternity. The time which he occupies in his public labours is the most valuable portion of our earthly existence—the sacred hours of the Sabbath and other select periods won from the multiplied cares and employments of life. To adapt his instructions to the circumstances and wants of every individual, to maintain constant and inviolable fidelity to him "whose he is, and whom he serves," and to enforce all his admonitions by the perpetual comment of a holy life are objects which demand his incessant attention. The responsibility which attaches to his person and exertions is ineffably great. Justly may any one tremble at the magnitude and obligations of such an office. The Apostle of the Gentiles, though he possessed a mind of unrivalled powers, and, with the clearest views and most mature Christian excellencies, enjoyed the rich gift of miraculous endowments, was constrained to exclaim, when he surveyed the requisitions and tendencies of his ministerial function, "Who is sufficient for these things?" To the ordinary sciences, arts, and avocations of human life, the ordinary powers and attainments of human nature may be equal: to the successful exercise of the Christian ministry something more is necessary. They who have used the greatest diligence and acquired the most estimable qualifications will be the first to acknowledge their entire dependence on the Holy Spirit's agency and to say, with the strongest emphasis of humble and prayerful feeling, "Our sufficiency is of God."

With such considerations as these the mind of David Stoner was deeply affected. He was fully convinced that a preacher of the gospel ought to be no novice in Christian experience or Christian wisdom; that to him all solid acquisitions are valuable, but a comprehensive, clear, and sound knowledge of sacred theology, indispensable; and above all, that he needs the "unction of the Holy One." To ascertain that he was called of God to this momentous employment caused him much painful and anxious inquiry; and this portion of his history affords an example, equally interesting and instructive, of the secret workings of a serious mind in the prospect of the most serious of all engagements—cautious in its deliberations, slow in its movements, but ultimately firm in its decisions.

Early in life he appears to have had a persuasion that, if faithful to the grace of God, he should eventually be called to the service of the sanctuary. This persuasion became more lively and powerful amid the religious exercises which engaged his attention, first at Barwick and afterwards at Rochdale. His most intimate associates thought they could then discover in him the elements of an able and useful minister of Jesus Christ. To himself, however, his invincible timidity seemed to present an insuperable objection. He therefore concealed the desires and predilections of his heart: he durst not think it possible that such a one as he should ever fill a station so honourable and arduous as that of the ministry; but at the same time he was led imperceptibly to pursue that course of study and spiritual discipline which served gradually to prepare him for the profitable discharge of its duties.

The first time any notice presents itself in his epistolary correspondence of the impression which he secretly cherished is in his letter to Mr. Gregory, partly quoted already, of June 9th, 1810. "I have *something*," he says, "continually on my breast. Perhaps you may recollect my timid spirit; but as you are a bosom friend, I will tell it you. It is this: something suggests, 'Go and preach the gospel;' but whether it be self, Satan, or the Spirit of God, how can I discover? Sometimes the thought arises, How can it be *self* when I am of so backward a disposition? How can it be *Satan?* Surely he would wish no man to preach.' But O! what must I do? Give me your advice. I hope you will disclose the above to no one."

His friend replied and made some observations on the subject of his inquiry. To him Mr. Stoner writes again in the month of September, expresses his gratitude for the advice he had received, and mentions the growing conviction he felt of the importance of the work which he contemplated—a conviction much strengthened by his reading a short essay on the "Qualifications and Duty of a Christian Minister," extracted from Dr. Bates.[1] "I know," he adds, "if the Lord has designed me to preach the gospel, he will open the way for me; but I fear I have rejected an offer at least once. Every day I more and more see my own ignorance, weakness, and insufficiency for such a work; but I know God is all wisdom, strength, and sufficiency, and he can impart these blessings to me. If I ask him in a proper manner, I believe he will do it; for it is his word, 'If any of you lack wisdom, let him ask of God, that giveth to all men liberally, and upbraideth not; and it shall be given him.' I heard Mr. Marsden on Wednesday evening from, 'Whatsoever ye shall ask the Father in my name, he will give it you.' I was much encouraged under this sermon. I well remember the observation of a literary and pious gentleman on the subject of asking wisdom. 'If,' said he, 'you ask wisdom of God, he will give you a little; and if you make good use of that, he will give you a little more; and so on in proportion.' And if God has given me a little, and I make no use of it, I tremble at the idea! What! hiding my talent in a *clean* napkin! God forbid! May he teach me wisdom secretly."

---

[1] See the *Methodist Magazine* for October and November, 1810.

Shortly after this he was seized with a dangerous fever which reduced him to a state of great debility. When he was recovered, he wrote again to his correspondent at Nottingham, February 13th, 1811, and adverted to the ends which he supposed his heavenly Father might have in view in afflicting him: to make him more thankful for the blessing of good health, to increase his love to himself, and, perhaps, to chasten him for not yielding to his convictions and beginning to preach. "For he showed me," he observes, "how easily he could take all my powers entirely away. I have not yet begun, and know not what to do. I have such a continual struggle in my poor soul between two contending parties (but who they are I know not), one pushing this way, the other pulling quite the contrary, that sometimes when it is suggested, 'Give it entirely up,' I almost think of listening to the suggestion. My natural temper is so opposed to such an office; I am so timid and diffident that to think of *preaching* makes me stagger and shrink from the duty. Perhaps you would advise me to mention the subject to some of the friends at Leeds: but that is what in me 'human nature trembles at.' After many mature considerations, however, I came to the resolution of naming it to my master and Mr. Lord, but 'under a mantle.' An opportunity offered itself. Mr. Sigston asked me one evening what were my intentions as to future life. I said, 'I have thought something about being a church minister; but I suppose, as I am circumstanced, that it is nearly impossible.' No more passed at that time; but afterwards he advised me, first, to examine what my reasons were for desiring to be a minister, and then to ascertain where it seemed most probable that I was called to exercise my ministry. This I have endeavoured to do, but have not yet had an opportunity of stating to him my conjectures upon the subject. I have since laid open my mind to Mr. Lord and desired him to speak to Mr. Sigston for me; but he has not yet done it. So here I am at a stand! quite unhappy! My eternity of happiness is diminishing! I am neglecting my duty, and my soul is at stake! Lord, help me!"

He then recites the examination into which he had entered of his views and motives in reference to the ministry. This turns chiefly on the two points suggested by Mr. Sigston. The importance of the following extract will, it is presumed, abundantly justify its length:

"First. What are the reasons that induce me to think of preaching? The glory of God, the benefit of my fellow-creatures, and the salvation of my own soul.

"1. The glory of God. Men were made to glorify God; but Adam fell into sin and has entailed his sin upon all his posterity. Of ourselves, therefore, we cannot glorify God. But Christ has died for us; and through his blood, and that alone, we may glorify God. Men, however, naturally dishonour God as much as lies in their power: they trample upon the Saviour's blood as an unholy thing. Now, can I in any way glorify God more than by becoming an instrument in his hands to induce souls to turn from their wicked ways and live to his glory? Besides, God has appointed a station for every man he sends into the world; and, consequently, one for me. I conceive that it is scarcely, if at all, possible that a man should properly glorify God out of that station which is designed for him. If then God has designed me to be a preacher of his gospel, I think I can scarcely, if at all, glorify him if I be not one.

"2. The benefit of my fellow-creatures. God made men not only to glorify him but to be eternally happy. But they have wandered from his ways 'like lost sheep.' They are 'taken captive by the devil at his will.' They feed upon the husks and shells of the wilderness. They are blind and poor, wretched and miserable, deaf and dumb; nay, more, they are 'dead in trespasses and sins.' God himself says, 'There is no peace to the wicked: they are like the troubled sea, when it cannot rest, whose waters cast up mire and dirt.' Besides all this, there is a 'fearful looking for' of eternal punishment and woe. This, if God's grace prevent not, is the lot of all the children of Adam. Can I then be more beneficial to my fellow-creatures than by being employed to let them know the day of their salvation? I could wish all men to be happy. I could wish all men to glorify God, to live a life of peace on earth, and at last to reign with him in the heavenly regions for ever and ever. When I look round on the world, lying, comparatively speaking, in the arms of the wicked one; when I see men sinful and wretched, and consider that many, many know it not, my heart yearns over them, and I would fain be instrumental in doing them good.

"3. The salvation of my own soul. In my present state of mind I am quite miserable. I think (right or wrong I know not), while I have so strong a conviction that I ought to preach, and preach not, I cannot be saved, for this reason: I think it is my duty; I do not perform my duty; how then can I expect salvation? I am so uneasy and unsettled, I have such a burden upon my spirit that sometimes I am almost ready to give all up. Lord, help me! Ever since I first set out in the ways of religion, the ministry has in general been the first thing in my thoughts. Before I went to Rochdale, when there was a revival of religion among the youth of my native village, and we often met together, I was the *preacher* for them. What happy days were those! Besides, what I consider as most decisive, when I live nearest to God and enjoy most of his love, *then,* and *then only* do my desires after the ministry increase. On the contrary, when I am cold and languid, my desires become weak and drooping. But what shall I do? Perhaps you have read the first part of the memoir of Mr. Robert Lomas.[1] I thank God that I have received much benefit from it. He seems to have been of the like disposition with me. He observes that he had 'openings of the Word of God to his mind and plans of discourses often presented.' That is just my case. Now I think I have mentioned all my reasons for wishing to be a preacher. Please to give me your opinion. Are they sufficient or are they not? I wish Mr. Sigston knew them as well as you now do. I thank God that I am able to declare my mind so fully to you. But you are at a great distance from me; and of all friends, I would soonest state my feelings to the most distant. I think you have no acquaintance at Leeds to whom you could reasonably and wisely mention this subject.

"Secondly. I am to ascertain, if I can, where it is most probable that I am called to exercise my ministry. On this point I fancy I need not study much. There are only two religious communities to which I can conscientiously unite myself: the Methodists and the established

---

1 The memoir of Mr. Lomas, an uncommonly interesting and edifying piece of Christian biography, is inserted in the *Methodist Magazine* for January, February, March, and April, 1811.

church. The question is, Which shall I choose? You may think it impracticable that one in my humble circumstances of life should become a minister of the establishment. I doubt not, however, that if I were fully bent upon it, I could manage that point."

He then repeats the reasons, mentioned above, which induced him to think of the ministry, and particularly inquires whether, in his case, he should have the fairest prospect of glorifying God, of promoting the spiritual interests of his fellow-creatures, and of securing his personal salvation as a clergyman of the establishment or a minister in the Methodist Connexion. The result is that he modestly but firmly gives the preference to the Methodist Connexion. "Besides," he subjoins, "if I go to the university in order to my becoming a minister of the establishment, my powers must be dormant until I am twenty-three years of age; whereas, among the Methodists, I might be instrumental in the conversion of many souls before then. But I have an unquenchable desire placed in me after learning; and if I went to the university, I should have a far better opportunity of obtaining literary qualifications than I can expect among the Methodists. But what is that? Comparatively nothing in the sight of God."

After this careful investigation of his principles and motives, it might be expected that he would immediately make trial of his abilities for the pulpit. Timidity, however, again prevailed and painfully retarded his purposes. He suffered peculiar disadvantages from that excessive reserve which would not allow him freely to unbosom his mind to others. About this time he prepared a letter to a great and good man, in which he stated his feelings, and particularly asked from what source the inclinations he had could arise? Did they spring from *self*? He thought they might, for he was *proud*. He thought, again, they did not; he was so *timid*. Did *they* spring from Satan? He saw it was possible that the devil might stimulate one to run who was not sent. Did they come from the Holy Spirit? This was the question he wanted solving. But when he had written his letter, he had not courage to send it. It was an additional inconvenience to him that he was now deprived of the society of Mr. Lord, who at the midsummer of this year quitted Mr. Sigston's, and shortly afterwards entered into the regular ministry.

In a letter to Mr. Gregory, dated July 5th, he says, "I very much admire your fine remarks on the pleasure of conveying our thoughts to each other, though at a great distance. This I think an inestimable blessing. You write, 'I hope I am endeavouring to live in an increasing conformity to the will of God.' Well, I can only say, Go on, and prosper; for this is the very end for which you were created. With regard to myself, I have but very poor news. I have not begun to sound the gospel trumpet, and I think now I never shall. I am still strongly persuaded that the call was from God; but, through my resisting the impulse, it has now almost quite left me; and consequently my soul is more dead, lifeless and carnal than it has ever been since I was brought out of 'darkness into light.' I fear I shall never hold up my head more. I have been of late so tossed and tempted, that I am now so melancholy and dejected, that I sometimes think I shall lose my reason. Lord God of heaven and earth, have mercy upon me! My two great hindrances are *timidity* and *pride*. I beg you will write soon and say something that may benefit me. I am spending the vacation," he adds in a postscript, "at Mr. Sigston's, as he is from home. We have three young men in the house who are going to Sierra-Leone under the direction of Dr. Coke to teach the heathen; so I am desired to stay here and teach them. The Lord of heaven and earth have mercy upon me!"

By the repeated persuasions of Mr. Sigston and several other friends he at length consented to make an attempt, and preached his first sermon in a small schoolroom in Park Lane, Leeds, October 17th, 1811, from Prov. 18:24: "There is a friend that sticketh closer than a brother." Contrary to his expectation, there was a considerable congregation, among whom were several local preachers. He felt much confusion and embarrassment and was greatly discouraged. Three days afterwards, however, he was induced to accompany Mr. Sigston and his friend Mr. Dobson to Kirkstall Forge, where Mr. Sigston had been appointed to preach. Mr. Stoner consented to supply for him; but on approaching the pulpit, his courage seemed to fail him and, observes Mr. Sigston, "perceiving him about to retire, I stepped forward and with some difficulty got him into the pulpit: so that it may be said of him, with even literal truth, that he was *thrust out* into the harvest." At this time he preached from John 9:27: "Will ye also be his disciples?" and experienced somewhat more freedom than he had done on the former occasion. To Mr. Gregory he writes on the 24th of the same month, "I find it is a great blessing to have friends to whom we can open all our minds and from whom we can receive Christian advice and consolation. Such a friend have you been to me; and as I shall never be able to make a suitable return, I most ardently pray that the choicest of God's blessings may rest upon you in life, death, and to all eternity. I have something to relate which, I dare say, will please you. I have taken your advice concerning my call to the ministry. I have made the attempt. I preached the first time in a small Sunday school room in an obscure part of the town. I did it as secretly as possible; but, to my great astonishment, seven or eight local preachers were present; on which account, through the weakness of my faith and trust in God, I did not feel that liberty and composure of mind which I expected; at which I was greatly cast down and disconcerted. My friends, however, expressed their satisfaction; and by their encouragement I went with Mr. Sigston to a small village on the Sabbath and stood up again, when I experienced more liberty and power, and the blessing of the Lord attended his Word. But O! what cogitations and imaginations have since passed through my mind! I am still scarcely satisfied whether it be the will of God or not that I should engage in the ministry. A thought strikes me," he remarks, "while I am writing. Perhaps if we were to meet in the streets, we should not know each other. We are changeable and changing. Dear sir, do not forget to pray, and for *me*. I often remember you."

His friends rejoiced that he had been prevailed upon to make a trial; and with the concurrence of a meeting of the local preachers, he received a note from the Rev. James Wood, then superintendent of the Leeds Circuit, authorizing him to exercise his talent for preaching the gospel and requesting the people to encourage him in his labours and pray for his success. Outlines of his first two sermons are extant, from which it is plain, to adopt the language of Mr. Lord, "that they were very instructive and awakening, crowded with important sentiments, though perhaps not displaying that lucid order and copious argumentation so conspicuous in his more matured compositions." He was, however, overwhelmed with discouragement, and for *four months* durst not venture again to enter the pulpit. At length he was constrained to make another effort. "I found," says he in a letter to Mr. Gregory of March 7th, 1812, "that I could not live. I was going, fast going down the stream of delusion and vanity. I summoned courage to try other twice the last two Sundays: but I feel, O! I feel unutterable pangs. When I stand up, my limbs tremble, my voice falters, my ideas are confused, and all my faculties of body and soul seem to be convulsed. But, thanks to God! he stands up with me; gives me tolerable liberty of speech; blesses me in my own soul; and, as far as I can learn, favours me with some tokens of success among the people." It afforded his friends much satisfaction to find that he had resumed his pulpit labours. His note from Mr. Wood was renewed; and during the remaining part of the year 1812 he often preached in different places, with increasing comfort to himself and advantage to his hearers.

It may not be improper to insert here his observations on the most satisfactory evidences of a call to the ministerial office, extracted from a letter which he wrote several years afterwards to Mr. Joseph Jennings; and a copy of which, with some other interesting documents, Mr. J. has kindly communicated to the writers of these pages. "You ask, 'What are the marks whereby a person may know that he is called of God to preach the gospel?' To make the matter as simple as possible, I would say,

"1. An inward impression on the mind made by the Spirit of God. This impression will lead you to think about preaching, texts, sermons, etc., and will be most vivid when you are most alive to God.

"2. The call of the church. Perhaps this will be known by some individuals inviting you to begin, and then by the *general* approbation and encouragement you will meet with after you have begun.

"But remember there must be a *fair trial*. You must preach *fifty* times before you conclude to give it up. And you must not be swayed by the opinion of *one* or *two* individuals, either *for* or *against*, but by the *general* opinion. I am fully satisfied that I am called of God; yet a good man, and a man of renown, expressed it as his opinion, after hearing my first sermon, that I was *not* called to the work. And you will soon ascertain the general opinion without making inquiries. Indeed, a man who makes inquiries how his hearers like his sermons is sure to be despised. By the invitations you receive, by the congregations you have, by the notice taken of you by the preachers, and by the uninvited opinions of some who will tell you what they think, you will soon ascertain the general opinion of the church.

"3. Success in your work. A preacher called of God must, in some way or other, have success. Nothing can satisfy a preacher of God's making and calling but *souls*. And 'he that winneth souls is wise.' You mention the acuteness of your feelings and distress of your mind. This, I think, is all in favour of your call. The torture of mind I passed through on that subject none but God Almighty knows. You must not be governed by your *feelings*, but by your *judgment*, making its decision according to the Word of God."

At the Christmas quarterly meeting of the same year, he was admitted as a probationer on the local preachers' plan for the Leeds Circuit. In a letter to Mr. Gregory, dated February 23rd, 1813, he complains that he is ignorant of himself, God, the Bible, the great work of preaching, and everything else that he ought to know; that his sermons are too frothy and light and contain too little of experience and the Word of God. His censure of himself, however, was always severe; and happily, the discouraging sentence which he pronounced was not supported by the suffrages of his hearers. He speaks no more of relinquishing his efforts, but expresses his intention, by the assistance of God, to try a little longer. He afterwards indulges in the following serious reflections: "How dreadful is our situation! Immortal worms, placed for a moment on the crumbling precipice of time, betwixt the two unbounded oceans of eternity! endowed with reason and free agency! born into the world, surrounded with darkness and ignorance! captivated by our lusts! possessed by Satan! allured by desires! deceived by prejudices! biased by sensual gratifications! led astray by example! and yet accountable for every thought, for every word, for every action! How great, how infinitely great is the blessing of early piety! Its advantages are inconceivable here below, but they will chiefly discover themselves throughout eternity."

In his next letter to the same friend, of April 1st, he speaks of his name having been inserted at a late meeting of the local preachers, on the list of reserve—as a proper person, we suppose he means, to be recommended in the regular way for the Wesleyan itinerancy. "I thank God," he subjoins, "that he yet enables me to speak a few words for him. I do not feel such a reluctance to ascend the pulpit as I used to do. My fear begins to wear off, and I am enabled to speak with more precision, firmness, and ease. But timidity and blushing backwardness are so deeply rooted in my nature that it will be with difficulty, if ever, that I get completely master of them. When I have liberty in the pulpit, I find preaching delightful work; but when I am embarrassed, I could wish myself almost anywhere out of the sight of the people. One thing I discover, that when I have an indifferent season, I can generally trace the cause of it to myself, and find it has arisen from my own fear, unbelief, forgetfulness, or indolence. I want direction from heaven concerning my future station and conduct in life. My heart is divided on the subject. One part suggests, 'Enter into a trade or something else of that kind.' Another says, 'Go out as a travelling preacher.' Now what am I to do? I wish to be as clay in the hands of the potter and say, 'Thy will be done.' I believe there is a certain track cut out for me in life by divine providence. If I enter upon and continue in this track, I shall be happy and successful; if I do not, all will be unfortunate and miserable. *Now I* want to see the designs of providence open before me, and *afterwards* I shall want strength to follow them. This placing me upon the list of reserve, is it an opening of providence or not? Pray what is the counsel of my friend on this important subject?"

On the necessity of seeking the constant aid of the Holy Spirit in the discharge of pulpit duty, he makes the following just and impressive observations in the same letter: "The greatest, the best, the most useful, the most necessary qualification for a preacher is the Spirit. Without the influence of the Spirit, sinners are crawling monsters, incarnate fiends; Christians are as a body without a soul; ordinances are fountains without water; ministers are windows without light; providences are clouds without rain; promises are trees without fruit. But with the Spirit, our prayers will be prevalent; our faith will be strong; our hope will be blooming; our love will be increasing; our preaching will be useful; our exhortations will be fiery; our consolations will be heart-easing; our warnings will be solemn; our reproofs will be pungent; our invitations will be encouraging; our introductions will be easy; our divisions will be natural; and our applications will be close. Thus, with the strength of God in our arms and the sword of the Spirit in our hands, we shall be enabled to cut and divide betwixt sinners and their sins; to lop off all useless and injurious branches; to cut off all right-hand sins; and thus the work of God will prosper in our hands. O let us, above every other, and with every other, qualification, seek the Spirit! Hear a preacher *without* the Spirit: you will find him dull, inactive, dead, useless—unless it be to talk people to sleep. His sermon is without *point,* without *edge.* In short, he is just the reverse of what I have been describing. But hear a preacher *with* the Spirit, and how contrary the effect! Though he may labour under disadvantages with regard to voice, manner, etc., yet you will perceive that he himself feels what he says, and you will feel it likewise. An unction will attend what he advances and bring it home warm to your conscience. Lord, give us the Spirit!"

"Some persons," he adds, "are of opinion that a preacher of the gospel ought to have nothing to do with the embellishments of oratory, etc. I think differently. I think we ought to seize every help, whether oratory, rhetoric, logic, or what not. Hence I would learn to read in the best manner; to speak and deliver what I have to say in the best manner; in short, to do everything in the best manner. Hence I should wish to acquire every attainment which may assist a minister to appear and acquit himself in the pulpit with advantage. Truly there is an extreme on the other side, in over-reaching the matter; but I think a speaker may proceed a long way before he approaches anything of that sort."

Mr. Lord correctly observes that Mr. Stoner was "from the first deeply convinced of the necessity of having 'beaten oil' for the sanctuary." He was, therefore, very diligent in his preparations for the pulpit. "There is a system," he remarks in one of his letters to Mr. L., "that some preachers whom I know frequently follow. They preach what I call *spun-sermons.* Mr.—, I should suppose, acts in this manner.

He is one of the most tedious preachers I ever heard. You may sit for a quarter of an hour while the poor man is puffing and blowing and tugging to get some idea thrown out to you; and when it does come, it is perhaps only what you have had before, or some idea which you might perceive to arise out of the passage with less than half a moment's consideration. He will begin a sentence, and before he gets halfway through it will meet with something that he supposes needs explanation; then he immediately enters the terrible enclosure of a parenthesis, and perhaps before he has half finished that explanation something else presents itself. He then turns his attention to it, and so goes on multiplying parenthesis within parenthesis, explanation of explanation, till he is completely lost in the labyrinth and gives up the chase. From such preaching, 'good Lord, deliver us.'"

From such preaching he was delivered. Knowing the value of close and persevering study, he laboured to be a scribe instructed unto the kingdom of heaven, "bringing forth out of his treasure things new and old." It was his endeavour that his sentiments should at once be valuable in themselves and correctly arranged. His sermons, therefore, were not a collection of excellencies thrown into a confused heap; his sentences were not pearls unstrung, which require considerable pains to collect and unite them in order to see their beauties. There was always a regular chain of argumentation in his discourses, where the first link naturally connected itself with the next, and that with the next, until he came to the conclusion.[1]

It will not escape the reader's notice that in examining his call to the ministry, Mr. Stoner invariably associated with his obedience to it a deep and painful solicitude for his personal salvation. This became a settled principle with him. He seems always to have thought that

---

1   On this subject it may not be unsuitable to introduce the following pointed remarks of the venerable Wesley, in his Notes on our Lord's Sermon on the Mount: "Through this whole discourse, we cannot but observe the most exact method which can possibly be conceived. Every paragraph, every sentence is closely connected both with that which precedes and that which follows it. And is not this the pattern for every Christian preacher? If any, then, are able to follow it, without any premeditation, well: if not, let them not dare to preach without it. No rhapsody, no incoherency, whether the things spoken be true or false, comes of the Spirit of Christ."

for a man to trifle with a serious conviction of the duty of engaging in the ministerial office was to endanger his spiritual interests. The following incident, related by the Rev. John Smith, may illustrate this. When Mr. Smith was employed as assistant in Mr. Sigston's academy, he was strongly induced to attempt pulpit labour, and consented to make a trial on a certain occasion.

His fears, however, overpowered him, and he did not attend the appointment. He made another engagement—to preach in Park Lane, where Mr. Stoner had commenced his public work; but as the time approached, he yielded again to timidity and retired to the teachers' room, intending not to make his appearance at the place appointed. Mr. Stoner was in the room. "I thought," said he to Mr. Smith, "that you had agreed to preach tonight."

"Yes," said the other, with much hesitation and embarrassment, "but I *must* give it up."

"What," rejoined Mr. Stoner, with severe and powerful emphasis, "do you mean then to *ruin* yourself?"

This pointed question, resting a compliance with acknowledged duty on a regard to personal safety, produced the desired result. Mr. Smith immediately repaired to Park Lane and there commenced those pulpit exertions which have been happily and successfully continued to the present time. To the most devoted ministers of Christ such a feeling as that above mentioned has been familiar; and they have been prompted to say, in humble imitation of the holy apostle, "Though we preach the gospel, we have nothing to glory of: for necessity is laid upon us; yea, woe is unto us if we preach not the gospel! For if we do this thing willingly, we have a reward: but if against our will, a dispensation of the gospel is committed unto us."

While Mr. Stoner pursued his occasional engagements as a local preacher, an opportunity seemed to present itself of his entering into an untried and most important field of action. Dr. Coke, who was then contemplating a mission to Ceylon and continental India, passed through Leeds, accompanied by Mr. Clough. He had heard of Mr. Stoner's piety and promising talent, and called upon him to secure his assistance as a missionary. When he found that Mr. Stoner understood the Portuguese language, he urged his request the more earnestly, observing that Mr. S. might afford himself and associates special assistance during the voyage. Mr. Stoner willingly acceded to the doctor's desire on condition that the full consent of his parents could be obtained. When they were consulted, Mrs. Stoner, who was both an affectionate and judicious woman, and uncommonly attached to her son David, could not give her approbation to the scheme, which was therefore abandoned. The judgment of this excellent mother appears to have been correct. It may reasonably be doubted whether the constitution of Mr. Stoner was at all adapted to a residence in an eastern climate, and whether his extreme diffidence would not have proved an insurmountable obstacle to many of the peculiar calls and engagements of an eastern missionary.

It was Mr. Wood's intention to propose him for the itinerancy in the year 1813. To this he objected, partly, as he observes in a letter to Mr. Lord, on the ground of his engagements with Mr. Sigston; and partly on account of his youth, the state of his health, his inexperience, his want of gravity, firmness, and competent ability. "I do not absolutely intend," he says, "not to go out. I thank God, I have studied over the matter, and just as I see that God opens the way, I trust I shall say, 'Thy will be done,' and follow." The objections which he advanced, the just grounds of some of which none but himself could discover, were overruled; and at the ensuing Conference his name appears to have been inserted on the president's list.

He was not called into the regular ministry, however, until the beginning of the year 1814, when he was directed to assist the Rev. Messrs. Morley, Bunting and Pilter in the Leeds Circuit. It was an arduous task to enter upon his more public office in the place where he had been trained and where he knew that a preacher's work was very difficult and trying; but he experienced the greatest kindness and consideration. His growing talents were properly and gratefully estimated, and his labours in this station were attended with much satisfaction to himself and spiritual profit to others.

Of his deportment during the period he spent at Leeds the Rev. George Morley, in whose house he resided, has communicated the following account: "Having had the most favourable opportunity of witnessing Mr. Stoner's spirit and conduct, I may say that he entered on his work with great fear and trembling, which arose from a sense of its vast importance and of his own insufficiency. But I can truly add, that his deep humility was never corrupted by a mixture of cowardice, nor did it ever prevent him from boldly declaring the 'whole counsel of God' in his public ministrations. His application to private duties was remarkably close, and his whole course of reading and study was pursued with a single eye to the glory of God. The effect of this was seen in the great congregation, where his profiting appeared unto all. In the commencement of his itinerancy he had many seals to his ministry, who both on earth and in heaven will declare him blessed. Such an entrance on his work raised high expectations concerning his future usefulness, which, I am persuaded, were fully realized."

The following solemn engagement is found on a small slip of paper, written most probably in the place where it is dated: "Hereby I, David Stoner, resolve, in the strength of my God, to love Jesus supremely, to serve him constantly, to follow him fully, to trust in him confidently, and to attend him closely; to delight in him only; to be his *now, henceforward,* and *for ever.* O God, pardon what is past, and help me for the future! Make me *holy* and *useful!*—David Stoner, Leeds Old Chapel, April 6th, 1814, being this day twenty years old." On the same paper he mentions the renewal of these holy purposes on two different occasions afterwards; and it will be discovered, from the subsequent part of his life, that they were never practically forgotten.

To some it may appear that Mr. Stoner was called too early into the full employment of the ministry. His, however, was a peculiar case. He possessed a maturity of mind, a depth of piety and a gravity of deportment seldom found at his age. Who that considers how short his career has proved will think that he commenced it too soon? His conduct ought to afford no encouragement to those who, immature in knowledge and experience as well as in years, deem themselves at once qualified for an office the high obligations of which they have never seriously considered. With such presumption and rashness David Stoner will not be charged. He always acted from conviction and proceeded with caution, presenting from the first ample promise of his future eminence. To him, in the successive stages of his ministerial course, may not unjustly be applied the highly figurative language which the Son of Sirach uses concerning Simon the High Priest: "He was as the morning star in the midst of a cloud, and as the moon at the full: as the sun shining upon the temple of the Most High, and as the rainbow giving light in the bright clouds: as the flower of roses in the spring of the year, as lilies by the rivers of waters, and as the branches of the frankincense tree in the time of summer: as fire and incense in the censer, and as a vessel of beaten gold: as a fair olive tree budding forth fruit, and as a cypress tree which groweth up to the clouds."[1]

---

1 Ecclus. 1:6–10.

4

Ministry at Holmfirth

He removes to the Holmfirth Circuit, where he zealously and successfully pursues his ministerial labours—Endangers his health by indiscreet exertion in the pulpit—Observations on this subject—A description of the place of his usual residence—His unabated conviction of the importance of the ministry—Extracts from his letters and diary—Anecdotes of an ignorant hearer, of an infidel, and of a miser—Takes his leave of his friends at Holmfirth and its vicinity with affectionate regret—Remarks on his diligent application to study.

At the Conference of 1814 he received an appointment to Holmfirth, near Huddersfield. In this peaceful retreat he spent two happy and prosperous years. His superintendent was the late Rev. John Brownell, a man for whom he entertained the most affectionate esteem, and with whom he deemed it a privilege to be associated in the same ministerial charge. Their attachment was mutual. They laboured together in uninterrupted harmony and parted with sincere regret. They have both now "accomplished their warfare" and doubtless renewed their intercourse in a brighter and better region.[1]

Mr. Stoner entered upon the duties of his new station with peculiar zeal and activity. The state of religion in different parts of the Circuit seems to have been comparatively low; and Mr. Brownell, who was afflicted with a severe attack of nervous fever, felt himself for some time unequal to his wonted exertions. Tokens of prosperity, however, soon appeared. Prayer-meetings were regularly established, believers were edified, and not a few instances occurred of sound and scriptural conversion. "Some of the most daring, hardened sinners in the Circuit," says Mr. Stoner in a letter to Mr. Sigston, "are

---

1 See an excellent memoir of Mr. Brownell from the pen of the Rev. Thomas Jackson in the *Wesleyan Methodist Magazine* for January, February, March, and April, 1823.

arrested by the word and brought to seek after God. These we receive as pledges of good, as welcome drops before the coming shower, as a hopeful presage of the coming torrent. In some places we have small revivals; in most there is a thirst for the word." The first time he preached at Holmfirth he selected for his text that appropriate passage, Acts 11:20-21: "And some of them were men of Cyprus and Cyrene, which, when they were come to Antioch, spake unto the Grecians, preaching the Lord Jesus. And the hand of the Lord was with them: and a great number believed and turned unto the Lord." A powerful influence appears to have accompanied this sermon. Many were affected, and among the rest, Miss Hannah Roberts, who was deeply convinced of her sin and want, and earnestly sought, until she happily found, the consolations and blessings of religion. She was afterwards united in marriage to Mr. Stoner, and for upwards of six years had faithfully shared his joys and sorrows when, by the mysterious appointment of divine providence, she finished her earthly course in the prime and vigour of life.

The exertions of Mr. Stoner were at first too great for his bodily strength. He began to discover painful symptoms of languor and infirmness, and became sensible that he must either change his mode of preaching or fall a sacrifice to his labours. His utterance, though distinct, was uncommonly rapid, his pauses short and few, and his sermons frequently long. It cannot be said that he fell into the error of those who draw their voice from the belly rather than from the lungs and throat. His speech flowed freely from its proper organs, but he expressed himself with extreme vehemence, and too much neglected the adaptation of the movements of the body to the various parts of a discourse, which serves so eminently to preserve a public speaker from injury and exhaustion. His friends remonstrated with him on these improprieties in his manner; but he replied that when he attempted to reform them, he almost invariably felt himself embarrassed; and, intent on doing present good, he, with pardonable but inconsiderate zeal, disregarded the consequences which threatened his own health and life.

In the end, however, he was convinced of his mistake, and endeavoured to correct it; but his habits were too strongly formed to do this entirely. To young preachers whom he saw exposed to the same danger he was ever ready to administer affectionate counsel; nor will it be unsuitable to introduce here the following admonitions, addressed to the Rev. Joseph Jennings, and expressive of his mature opinion on this subject: "Take care of your health. Do not shout and scream. Is it *strength* of *voice* that saves souls or the *influence of the Spirit?* If it is not *strength* of *voice*, do not kill yourself before the time. If you scream yourself into a consumption, who will thank you? Will the church of Christ? Will those who love you? Will those souls thank you that might have been saved by your longer life? Will Jesus Christ thank you? No, but devils may. Avoid a cough as you would avoid the plague. Take your work as you can bear it, especially till you get seasoned. Your body is the 'temple of the Holy Ghost.' Take heed you do not sap its foundation, injure its walls, destroy its furniture, or harm its roof. I heard a young man preach the other night who spoke with such rapidity that I never before saw so clearly the disadvantage and evil of speaking so fast. It appeared to me that the rapidity of the speaker completely prevented any impression from being made on the minds of the people. It was almost impossible for me to *think as* fast as he *talked;* and if this is the case with my preaching and yours, what good can we expect to do?"

To other young ministers in the Wesleyan Connexion the above remarks will not be inapplicable. Precluded by the customs of the body to which they belong from the use of notes in the pulpit, animated by zealous ardour in the declaration of truth, and endowed with too small a portion of that unembarrassed self-possession which persons more aged and experienced find it difficult at all times to maintain, it is not surprising that they are occasionally betrayed into intemperate and mismanaged exertions, neither safe for themselves nor beneficial to their hearers. The opposite extreme is perhaps still worse. A heavy and drowsy enunciation of the everlasting verities of holiness and mercy is intolerable. But surely a just medium may be observed. It was a saying of the Rev. Samuel Bradburn's that when he wished to be peculiarly energetic he generally endeavoured to be proportionally slow.

By a greater attention to his constitutional debility and to the manner of discharging his public duties, Mr. Stoner's health was soon recruited; nor does he appear to have found it necessary to desist from his ordinary labours. The situation in which he was placed was very salubrious—cold and exposed, indeed, in winter, but in spring and summer inexpressibly beautiful and romantic. The fresh mountain breezes seemed to infuse new vigour into his languid frame. Of his usual residence he gives the following account in one of his letters to Mr. Gilpin: "The scenes of my present stage of existence are friendly to reflection rather than description. My situation resembles the reign of some pacific sovereign. It is pleasant to live in, but its annals are not the most splendid to record. 'The periods which make life happy do not always render history brilliant.' I dwell in a snug retreat perched on the side of a mountain at the foot of which the river Colne winds through the valley. Between the river and the house in which I reside is the high road from Huddersfield to Buxton, etc. Before the door is a small garden, behind the house a beautiful walk in a grove, and beyond that, upon the top of the mountain, a large wood. Across the valley in front of the house is the side of another mountain, intersected with roads, inlaid with meadows, and bespotted with cottages. A little farther down in the valley is Holmfirth, a small village; but the neighbourhood is very populous. Our chapel is a large building, capable, I suppose, of holding sixteen hundred people. On the Sabbath it is delightful to see the people streaming down the hills on all sides and aiming at the different places of worship."

In this enviable retirement he cultivated a growing intercourse with God and diligently applied himself to his proper pursuits. Among his other engagements it was his custom to compose one new sermon every week and to read a portion of his Greek Testament daily. Here also he commenced, and successfully prosecuted, his study of the Hebrew language.

The frequency with which he was now employed in pulpit and pastoral duties served to increase rather than to diminish his conviction of the weight of the ministerial office—a conviction which, as Mr. Lord remarks, "gave energy and permanency to the glowing zeal which characterized his public labours." To this esteemed friend he writes, April 14th, 1815: "You observe, 'We are engaged in a most important work.' True, O brother! Enviable and yet awful employment! honourable and yet fearful! delightful and painful! How ennobling to be an 'ambassador for Christ;' and yet how afflictive to be to some the 'savour of death unto death!' How pleasing to rend the veil which separates heaven from earth and display to obedient believers the greatness of the glory which awaits them beyond the flood! But how terrible to open the doors of the bottomless pit and point out to rebellious sinners the blackness of the darkness, the intenseness of the torment, the eternity of the misery which attend them in the boundless, bottomless, endless lake 'which burneth with fire and brimstone!' What love, what humility, what courage, what faithfulness, what prudence, what zeal, what patience, what deadness to the world are necessary for the proper discharge of our ministerial duties! O may the God of all grace supply you and me with these qualifications!"

About the same time he writes to Mr. Gilpin: "Procrastination! Ah! what a thief is procrastination! Nothing is so great, nothing so insignificant, but this villain can lay his purloining hands upon it and stuff it into his monstrous bag, oblivion! He steals moments, minutes, hours, days, weeks, months, years, bodies, souls! From the account which you give me respecting yourself I derive both pleasure and pain—*pleasure* that you sometimes determine to lead a *new life*—*pain* that those determinations are not carried into practical effect. Jacob had two sons of vastly different characters. Of one it was said, 'Unstable as water, thou shalt not excel.' Of the other, 'Can we find such a one as this is, a man in whom the Spirit of God is? Joseph is a fruitful bough, even a fruitful bough by a well, whose branches run over the wall.' Which character is more worthy of imitation? Fickle Reuben or steadfast Joseph? My dear lad, let me recommend to you the 'one thing needful.' Remember, it is but *one* thing, religion! And it is *needful* to create constant pleasure, to secure blooming honours, to obtain durable riches; to afford support in the hour of death and enable you to triumph in the morning of the resurrection. Habitually accustom yourself to look at things with the eyes of a dying man and an immortal spirit. When you come to stand trembling upon the verge of an unknown eternity, just ready to wing your way into the world of spirits, how will this world appear then? Its brilliancies will fade; its imposing glare will be dispelled; its beauties and enjoyments will sink into insignificance. Take these views of the world *now* and exemplify their influence in your daily conduct. Youth is a slippery path. Sensible objects strike the flippant mind of the inexperienced youth with force; they arrest his attention and engage his heart. To the transitory scenes of time oppose the realities of eternity. Eternity! incomprehensible, dreadful, joyful word! Who can tell the length of eternity? We giddy, thoughtless creatures have begun an existence which must *never* end. Watch unto prayer. Never issue out of your chamber into the world, never retire to rest without supplicating the author of your being for his grace. Every day read more or less in that book of books, the Bible. And may the best blessings of 'Him that dwelt in the bush' attend all your steps!"

To Mr. Smith he writes, October 17th, of the same year: "All praise to the donor of every good and perfect gift, I continue to enjoy the blessings of health of body and peace of mind; and I am endeavouring so to conduct myself that these gifts may glorify the giver. We are doing nothing particular in the Circuit at present. We want a fresh gale of holy heavenly inspiration. 'Come from the four winds, O breath, and breathe upon these slain, that they may live!' It is four years this day since I preached my first sermon in Park Lane. How wonderfully has God conducted me from that time until now! O let us praise him for the past and trust him for the future! I hope you and Mr. Fletcher are going on well with preaching, declaring the essential doctrines of Christianity with simplicity and plainness, and with the 'Holy Ghost sent down from heaven.' I am more and more convinced that sermons alone cannot convert sinners. This is God's work. It is he who wounds and heals, who kills and makes alive."

In the year 1816 he began occasionally to insert notices of his religious experience and observations in a book which he kept for the purpose, and which, for want of a more appropriate term, we style his diary, though it by no means contains a *daily* record of his views and feelings. "Monday, January 1st," he writes, "God has spared me to see the commencement of another year. I would begin it with new resolutions to love him with my whole heart and to serve him with all my strength. Author of my being, and fountain of my blessings, renew my heart! This evening I received the sacrament and solemnly renewed my covenant with God. May it be ratified in heaven! I felt much of the power of God. Sunday, 7th. In preaching this day I have felt the consequences of 'quenching the Spirit' on Thursday. It has been a heavy, dull day. On hearing of a bad report falsely raised concerning me, I felt the risings of pride. Lord, deliver me! For a wonder, one or two sinners at Thong are under deep convictions. Sunday, 14th. In answer to prayer, this has been a good day. Sunday, February 25th. Preached at Holmfirth three times. Had a good day. Felt considerable enlargement of soul in the afternoon while speaking from, 'Almost thou persuadest me to be a Christian.'"

Sometimes he introduced into this record an account of remarkable occurrences which he had either personally witnessed or heard from others. A few of these are found at this period of his history. The three following, it is presumed, will not be thought utterly unworthy of notice, as illustrative of his observant habits and of the fatal principles which frequently operate in unenlightened and unrenewed human nature.

One of them forcibly represents the inattention with which a person may for years sit under the ministry of the gospel. "Friday, January 12th. I was sent for to see a sick old man who has regularly attended our chapel. I asked him if he had sinned against God. He answered that he had 'sometimes been conquered by passion, but had always been very careful about *sinning.*' I explained the nature and necessity of repentance and faith. He replied, 'I have *always* believed in that, thank God.' Such is the total ignorance of some who attend our preaching. Lord, help me henceforth to speak more plainly!" An important petition. To lower the sacred dignity of divine truth by coarse language and unseemly comparisons is highly censurable; but to state it in the plainest and most intelligible manner ought undoubtedly to be the constant aim of every Christian minister. "Discourse," says the most eminent of the ancient rhetoricians,[1]

---

1   Quintilian, quoted by Dr. Blair, in Lect. X.

"ought always to be obvious, even to the most careless and negligent hearer; so that the sense shall strike his mind, as the light of the sun does our eyes, though they are not directed upwards to it. We must study, not only that every hearer may understand us, but that it shall be impossible for him not to understand us."

The next fact we shall mention affords a distressing view of the envenomed influence of modern infidelity on the vicious and untutored mind. "Wednesday, February 28th. Heard this day of a Deist living near Wooldale who is afflicted. Two of his deistical companions went to see him, remained with him a considerable time, and exhorted him to keep up his spirits. He says 'he will never pray while breath is in his body.' One of our people met him at the door, walking with crutches. 'Now, Daniel,' says he, 'God has laid his afflicting hand upon you.' 'He comes to no thanks for that,' answered he. 'But he can afflict you more.' He cannot,' replied he, savagely. God, however, has made him know since then that he can." It is said of some that they shall "fret themselves, and curse their king and their God, and look upwards." How awfully is this often verified in the blaspheming infidel! He anticipates the rage and despair of his future pain. To the minister of Christ he ought to be an object of compassion and sorrow. His fault lies in his depraved heart rather than his understanding, and he needs the most earnest appeals and expostulations of injured truth.

A third instance which Mr. Stoner records exemplifies the nature and effects of that most pitiful and debasing malady, the love of money. "Friday, March 8th. Heard of a man of considerable property who lived and died near Honley. When he was near death, he ordered a bag of gold to be brought that he might look at it. He viewed it for some time with pleasure and then said, 'Put it under my pillow.' It was done. Afterwards, when he was dying, and could scarcely articulate, he faltered, 'Let me lift it once more.'" To such wretches the term *miser,* which properly signifies *miserable,* is justly applied. Money is their god, to which they attach themselves with all the pertinacity of canine madness. They cherish it as their all and part with it only with their lives. "Avarice," says a distinguished Latin historian,[1] "is the inordinate desire of money, which no wise man covets. As if imbued with noxious drugs, it effeminates the body and the mind of man. It is ever boundless and insatiable, nor is it diminished either by plenty or by want."

"Nothing," observes Cicero,[2] "is such a proof of a narrow and little mind as the love of riches. Nothing is more honourable and noble than to despise money, if you have it not; and, if you have it, to bestow it in acts of beneficence and liberality." On this subject, even Pagans, unenlightened as they were with regard to many vital points of truth and duty, could think with accuracy and speak with energy. The sentiments which they have uttered reprove multitudes who possess the rich boon of divine revelation. A far higher authority than theirs has said, "Charge them that are rich in this world that they be not high-minded, nor trust in uncertain riches, but in the living God, who giveth us richly all things to enjoy; that they do good, that they be rich in good works, ready to distribute, willing to communicate; laying up in store for themselves a good foundation against the time to come, that they may lay hold on eternal life."

Mr. Stoner quitted his delightful retirement at Holmfirth with unaffected regret. "Tuesday, August 13th," he writes, "I left Holmfirth Circuit. In it I have spent two happy years. I have never had one jarring string of any importance. And what is still better, God has given me many seals to my poor ministry. May I find them at his right hand! It is peculiarly painful to flesh and blood to leave this kind, affectionate people. How gladly could I live and die among them! But 'here we have no continuing city.' Mr. Brownell has been a very agreeable and affectionate superintendent, and I feel very loath to part with him."

The diligence with which he pursued his private studies during his residence at Holmfirth has already been mentioned. It deserves remark. From his remaining manuscripts, it is evident that he was at this time indefatigable in his application, and that he made considerable progress in theological knowledge as well as in other useful attainments. His principles were more fully established; the style of

---

1 Sallust, Bell. Catil., cap. 11.
2 De Officiis, lib. i.

his preaching was more exactly formed; and all his qualifications became better adapted to those more extensive scenes of ministerial labour which began to open before him. Aware that as he advanced in the itinerancy his official calls and engagements would multiply, and habitually active in all his mental endeavours, he seized upon this season of comparative vacancy to provide a stock of needful information against future exigencies. To young men who are commencing the years of their ministerial probation, his conduct furnishes a valuable precedent. Those years are inestimable. It is then that permanent acquisitions are made and suitable habits contracted. If such years pass away in negligence and sloth—if, from a mistaken notion that subsequent effort will supply the deficiencies of present inattention, they are employed in anything rather than the proper studies and exercises of the ministry—the issue must be barrenness, disappointment, and remorse. The flexibility of youth soon ceases; times of unbroken leisure depart as the "shadow of a cloud;" and the ill-qualified teacher of heavenly truth, baffled in his unwarrantable expectations, reaps the vanity which he has so indiscreetly sown.

5

Ministry at Huddersfield

He is stationed at Huddersfield—Extracts from his diary—His views of entire sanctification, which he earnestly desires—Still assiduous in his attention to pulpit duty—Part of a letter to Mr. Gilpin—Other extracts from his diary—Record of his diligence in reading and study—He is admitted into full connexion with the Methodist Conference—His marriage—More extracts from his diary—Remarks on his ministerial success and his religious experience during the period he spent at Huddersfield.

The talents and zeal of Mr. Stoner did not escape the attention of the Circuits adjoining to that in which he had recently laboured, and on his quitting Holmfirth he was gratefully received at Huddersfield, to which place he was appointed in the year 1816. Here he remained three years. His colleagues were, first, the Rev. George Sargent, whose lamented death, by the overturning of a coach, occurred in the same neighbourhood a few years afterwards,[1] and the Rev. James Sykes; and then the Rev. Thomas Cooper and the Rev. John Hanwell; with the last of whom he subsequently maintained a free and friendly correspondence.

During his residence at Huddersfield he attended more frequently than before to his diary, in which he inserted larger notices of his religious experience. From these we shall furnish extracts. They will sufficiently attest the care and vigilance which he employed in the duty of self-examination; the growing desires which he cherished for the full attainment of Christian purity; the fidelity which he preserved in the performance of his ministerial functions; and the severity with which he passed sentence on his own deficiencies. This was undoubtedly, in many instances, excessive; but its very excess proves how solicitous he was in all things to approve himself unto God.

---

1   A short but very interesting memoir of Mr. Sargent is inserted in the *Wesleyan Methodist Magazine* for February, 1824.

"August 24th, 1816. I this day enter on my new Circuit with much 'fear and trembling.' What shall I do! I feel very uncomfortable; and yet I derive some support from a promise which I received two or three weeks since, while praying at Thong: 'My presence shall go with thee, and I will give thee rest.'

"Tuesday, October 8th. I have now been six weeks in the Circuit. I had not heard of any awakenings and was beginning to fear that God had forgotten to be gracious. But, praise to his name! I learned on Sunday at Linthwaite that a woman was convinced of sin the first day I was in the Circuit; and today I was informed of a backslider's being awakened at Honley. To God be all the glory! I am much troubled with fickleness of mind. Lord, help and save me!

"Thursday, November 14th. I feel cold and languid and indifferent. I yesterday proved a rebel, and yet I have not that humiliation and contrition which I desire. Lord, subdue my proud heart!

"Monday, December 2nd. I yesterday had a good day. I have felt some quickening influences a few days past. I want a *clean heart*. What pride and self do I find lurking in my best actions! 'Create in me a clean heart, O God; and renew a right spirit within me!'

"Wednesday, 4th. This evening I solemnly renewed my covenant with God. I gave him my body, my soul, and my all. I felt a softening of heart, but did not receive any particular token that God had accepted the offering. Elijah presented the sacrifice; he then prayed; and then followed the acceptance and the token of the acceptance—the fire from heaven. This is what I want. I feel the need of a clean heart. Pride and envy I can discover in myself continually. I believe God is able and willing to deliver me. And I am determined to seek the blessing with my whole heart. But at the same time, I think pride is in my motive. 'Do what I will, it haunts me still.' It is the fly in the pot of ointment. Lord, save me!

"Tuesday, 17th. I still am seeking after the great blessing, though sometimes disheartened, and sometimes tempted to relapse into my former state of indifference. Yet I am determined to pursue. I want more spiritual-mindedness. I want continually to *see* and feel the presence of God. I can often spend many minutes, yea, not infrequently, an hour, and never advert to God. I want a *habit* of living by faith. I have been examining myself and reviewing my past life. Besides those mercies which are common to many of my fellow-creatures, I have had 'some particular personal blessings, which ought to excite special thankfulness.' 1. I was born in an enlightened age and gospel land, of pious Methodist parents, from whom I received many instructions, reproofs, and corrections in my early days. 2. I had the opportunity of sitting under an able and powerful ministry. 3. I enjoyed the early influences of saving grace. 4. I was sent to Mr. Bridge's at Rochdale, where I was enabled to make some advancement in learning. 5. As soon as I left school, I had an opening at Leeds into a religious and suitable family. 6. Though often lukewarm and careless, yet I never ceased meeting in class. 7. *Early, loud, long,* and at last *obeyed,* calls to preach. 8. As soon as I was free from my engagement with Mr. Sigston, I was taken into the Leeds Circuit. 9. I enjoyed the blessing of God on my unworthy labours in the Holmfirth Circuit, so that many were awakened. And yet there are many evils under which I have daily to groan. 1. Excessive natural timidity, bashfulness, or false modesty, so that I am sometimes ready to prefer strangling to the performance of some duties, which to many are no trouble at all. 2. The little success I have had in my present ministerial labours. I have heard of only two awakenings since I came into this Circuit. 3. I have complaints from the people that I do not visit them sufficiently. 4. Instability of character—too much of Reuben. 5. A wicked, worldly, proud, peevish, impatient, selfish heart. 6. Non-improvement of much precious time. Lord, help me!

"January 1st, 1817. Last night I preached at the watch-night at Barwick. I praise God for all the blessings of the past year, and desire to begin a new year with a *new heart.*"

To the entire renewal of his soul in "righteousness and true holiness" his attention was now particularly directed. It was a source of much concern to him that, in the parts where he had lately laboured, this inestimable blessing seemed too generally disregarded. To quicken himself in the pursuit of it, and to recommend it to others, he about this time composed and preached a sermon on Christian perfection, an outline of which has been found among his papers. The materials are professedly taken in a great degree from the writings of Mr. Wesley, but the whole is evidently studied with much care. The explanatory part is distinct and satisfactory, and the arguments by which the doctrine is enforced are powerful and convincing.

Of this momentous subject he often speaks in his subsequent correspondence. The two following extracts may not improperly be introduced here as containing his mature and settled judgment. The first is taken from a letter addressed to Mr. Joseph Jennings in the year 1823.

"You ask various questions concerning sanctification. By 'sanctification' I suppose you mean what Mr. Wesley terms '*entire* sanctification.' Sanctification begins in justification; *entire* sanctification is Christian perfection. You ask,

1. 'Does it cause as great a change in the mind as justification does in the conduct?' If I rightly understand what you mean by this question, I would say, No. Justification, which is always accompanied by regeneration, is a change from *nature* to *grace;* entire sanctification is rising from a *lower* to a *higher degree* of grace. The former is a transition from *darkness* to *light;* the latter is rising into *clearer* light.

2. 'After the reception of perfect love, is there a constant evenness of mind; or is the soul liable to doubtfulness, oppression, and sorrow?' Certainly the soul is capable of sorrow. Look at Jesus: he was *angry,* he was *grieved,* he *wept,* etc. Yet it is a sorrow compatible with unceasing joy. 'As sorrowful, yet always rejoicing,' says the apostle. And the soul may also be liable to doubtfulness, though perhaps the source of that doubtfulness is in the individual himself. Entire sanctification may be wholly lost; and if so, it may be partially lost. The believer may hold it with a trembling hand. There are many stages between *no faith* and *full assurance.*

3. 'Is not our own will the greatest of all obstacles to the renewing of the soul in righteousness?' Undoubtedly:

> The hindrance must be all in me;
> It cannot in my Saviour be;
> Witness that streaming blood!

4. 'Does the enjoyment of entire sanctification enable us to pray, believe, and rejoice every moment, even in the presence of the greatest trials?' Doubtless, so far as it is *naturally,* or perhaps I should say *physically,* possible.

5. 'Does it enable us to seek only the glory of God, and are our wills lost at all times in his will?' Certainly, so long as perfect love fills and rules the heart. Do not set the mark too high. It is nothing but *love*. It is a very simple thing. *Plead* for it. *Wrestle, agonize* for it. *Believe* for it. Believe *just now*. If it is to be had by faith, it is to be had *just now*."

The second extract is from a letter written in the year 1820 to a friend who had lost the evidence of his sanctification, and who anxiously inquired by what means he might recover it. It will not be forgotten that Mr. Stoner is speaking of sanctification as it consists of loving God with the whole heart. Advancement in Christian *knowledge* and Christian *practice* is, in the nature of things, progressive and indefinite. A person too who at present loves God with all his soul is capable of a continual enlargement of his powers and consequently of a continual increase of love. Through eternity itself the happy saint, who rejoices in brighter effusions of light issuing from its eternal and inexhaustible source, and employs himself in stronger ascriptions of praise to the adorable Trinity, will doubtless experience also a perpetual and inconceivable augmentation of his love.

"You ask, 'What must I do? I have lost the blessing of sanctification.' I answer, *'Believe* in the Lord Jesus Christ, and thou shalt be saved.' It appears to me, 1. That you have a conscience not only *tender* but *scrupulous*, excessively *sore;* and, 2. That you rob yourself by *reasoning* instead of living by *faith*. As to the instance you mention, by which you lost the blessing, I question, 1. Whether you did not condemn yourself where God did not condemn; and, 2. If it should be true that you were guilty of unfaithfulness, you should have immediately humbled yourself, applied by faith to the blood of sprinkling, and prayed for grace to be more faithful in future. You ask, 'Did you ever feel in the same manner?' I answer, Yes, many a time. You ask, 'How must I proceed? Must I *fast* much?' I answer, No. Your body is the 'temple of the Holy Ghost;' and it is at your peril if you undermine the foundation or injure the walls of that temple. *Fast* and *abstain* you may and should; but not in any degree so as to *injure* your body, but *govern* it; 'for no man ever yet hated his own flesh, but nourisheth and cherisheth it.' In order to obtain the blessing again, the command is not, Pray much, fast much, weep much; but, Believe: '*only* believe; all things are possible to him that believeth.' Now, in this instant, while this paper is in your hand, hear the Saviour's voice, 'I will, be thou clean.' Believe it, venture, dare, try to believe, and the work is done. Remember, the Saviour is infinitely desirous to save you to the uttermost *just now*. Then what shall hinder? 'Lord, here I am. I give up all. I am fully thine. Thou art my Saviour. I will, I do believe!' Hallelujah! Bless the Lord! It is the devil who tells you, you ought not to preach till you have received the blessing again. He would be glad enough to shut your mouth. Preach on, and preach that blessing till you get it, and then you will preach it because you have it. You say, 'This is the second *time* I have lost it.' And what then? If it were the thousandth time, still the command *is, Believe.* You ask, 'Must I tell others that I have lost it?' I would say, generally, this would be very improper. It would weaken the feeble-minded and stagger those who are seeking. You know we are to preach not our own experience but the whole counsel of God. If you have an intimate friend or two, you might tell them: they would help you by their prayers, etc. Do not write bitter things against yourself. Begin from this hour, and spend all that time in *praising* that you have been wont to spend in *complaining,* and I am sure your soul will rise." From this letter the person to whom it was sent gratefully acknowledged that he derived much instruction and encouragement.

Mr. Stoner's ardent desires after the full renovation of his nature rendered him still more assiduous in the discharge of his public duties and in the acquisition of every profitable attainment. In a letter to Mr. Smith, dated January 17th, 1817, in which he particularly adverts to the subject of Christian holiness, he mentions also the satisfaction he had received from a perusal of Dr. Cotton Mather's *Student and Preacher*. The following sentences he transcribes: "Entertain the people of God with none but well-studied sermons; employ none but well-beaten oil for the lamps of the golden candlestick. This

I insist upon, that, when you are to preach, you should go directly from your knees in your study to the pulpit." These directions were conscientiously followed by Mr. Stoner. In him diligence of preparation and prayerful reliance on divine aid seemed equally united.

Under the same date he writes to Mr. Gilpin "A little time ago we wrote 1816, but now it is 1817. This indicates that time is flying, that eternity is approaching, and that we have entered upon a new portion, a new division, of our existence. Among the many practical uses which arise out of this distribution of our time, this is one, and not one of the *last* or *least*, that it affords us an opportunity, and loudly calls upon us, to settle our accounts, to close our books, to examine into our circumstances and ascertain whether we are gaining or losing. This is the conduct of the tradesman; and this should be the conduct of the moralist, the philosopher, the scholar, and the Christian. This I have been endeavouring to do. You give me the pleasing information in your last that you have begun to meet in class. I am exceedingly glad to hear it. Meeting in class has been much declaimed against; but it is a practice so clearly established by Scripture precepts and Scripture precedents—in *principle* at least, if not in *form*—a practice pregnant with so many advantages, productive of such blessed results, and enforced by so many powerful motives, that no man who wishes to glorify his Maker and save his own soul can justly incur censure by uniting himself in this way with the people of God. If you wish to enjoy the full influence of religion, if you wish to persevere to the end, *regularly attend your class.* Whether you be cold or hot, languid or alive, *go!* Let nothing prevent you from attending that ordinance of grace, and you will find it useful. In the temperament of your mind I think I remember three conspicuous features: *ambition, fire,* and *levity.* Your *ambition* and *fire* restrain in a due degree, direct them to proper objects, get them sanctified by divine grace; and then you will find them of wonderful use in carrying you through life. Let the object of your *ambition* be to become one of the wisest, the best, the holiest, the most useful of your species; and let the *fire* of your constitution prompt you to employ every means to conquer every enemy, to surmount every obstacle in the attainment of your object. But beware of *levity! It* will be 'a worm i' th' bud.' Let not

Satan deceive you by calling it Christian cheerfulness. Levity is not cheerfulness, though perhaps in their utmost boundaries they may appear to meet. Above all, *pray, pray, pray*. Do not suffer yourself to be satisfied with cold, short, infrequent prayers. As you pray, so will your soul prosper or decline. As you pray, so will you live."

From his diary it appears that he still kept the important object of holiness in view, but that he had many fluctuations in his religious experience. "February 13th," he writes, "I am still aiming at the great blessing, a clean heart; but O! how sluggish I am!" This seems to have been his general feeling and complaint. It will be proper, however, to insert his own language more at large.

"Tuesday, July 8th. When I consider that I am a Methodist, a professor of religion, nay, a minister of Christ; and when I look at my past conduct and experience, 'shame ought to burn my cheek to cinder.' I have been living for a considerable time at a poor, cold, dead rate. But, I thank God, I feel revived once more. I had a pretty good day on Sunday. Yesterday evening I had a season like one of those times of old when the 'candle of the Lord shone upon my head!' I feel at present a nearness to God, and I hope I shall not rest till I obtain the 'fulness of God.' O my God, I can appeal with sincerity to thee. 'I would be thine, thou know'st I would.' Come and fill me with thyself!

"Monday, 14th. It was suggested to me last week that my present fit of earnestness would soon be over, like all that had gone before. But, I thank God, it is not over yet. But O! what a hard heart I have! God has in part answered my prayers and given me to see a small degree of my spiritual corruption. My soul is full of vain, proud, selfish thoughts, envious thoughts, wandering thoughts, wicked thoughts. Pride enters into and spoils every duty, every action. Lord, save me!

"September 9th. The time which has elapsed since I entered anything into this journal proves that all has not been right. I lost ground at the Conference by not having time and opportunity for the regular performance of private duties and, in consequence, falling into idle conversation. I had, notwithstanding, a pretty good time in preaching at the Conference, and several profitable seasons in preaching in my native place and its vicinity. But since I returned to this town, my soul has been in a wretched condition. I know not what to do. I know I cannot deliver myself. None but God can do it. This deliverance can be obtained only by the earnest prayer of faith. And yet I cannot pray. Such is my state of listlessness. Lord, have mercy upon me!

"March 27th, 1818. Irresolution is my bane. How exactly do I resemble Reuben—'unstable as water!' Confident I am I cannot 'excel.' I do not excel in *knowledge*—darkness rests upon my mind; in *holiness*—I am a sinner; in *usefulness*—I am a mass of corruption, exhaling pestilential steams. In *everything* I am 'as a beast' before God. But I must not lie where I am. Up, and be doing!

"Monday, April 6th. I have now been in the world twenty-four years. God has given me, during this period, health, food, raiment, habitation, the comforts of life, kind friends, his Word, his Spirit, every blessing, every opportunity, every favour. But O! what returns! What ingratitude! What lukewarmness! What coldness! Lord, humble my proud heart! I am the foulest of the foul, the vilest of the vile, the 'chief of sinners.' But, there is a Mediator. O that I could come to him! I cannot feel. I cannot pray. I cannot mourn. Lord, break this rocky heart! I have made in days past ten thousand vows and formed ten thousand resolutions; and as often have they been broken. But I must come again. I want to give God my heart, but I feel as if I could not do it. So listless! So cold! Even while I am now engaged in this solemn duty, my heart is wandering to the ends of the earth! Lord, have mercy upon me! I think I am willing, by the grace of God, to give up every idol—to surrender everything into the hands of my Redeemer. Lord God Almighty! if there is anything within me which I do not see, and which prevents me from rising into liberty, show me the idol! Help me to hate, help me to surrender it; and help me *now!* But yet there is no feeling! Alas! what is knowledge without feeling! What is light without warmth! Come, O Jesus, and melt my hardness into love!"

On the 8th of April, the same year, the foundation of the present large and elegant chapel at Huddersfield was laid. Mr. Stoner mentions the circumstance and devoutly prays "that God would bless the intended erection and render it conducive to the salvation and happiness of thousands."

"Tuesday, 28th," he proceeds, "Blessed be God that yesterday I felt the Holy Spirit softening and drawing my heart. How often has biography proved a peculiar blessing to my soul! When I read the lives of Baxter, Fletcher, Wesley, Alleine, Pearce, Lomas, Spencer, etc., I am melted, I am ashamed, I am humbled, I am all on fire! But O! this instability! this want of firmness in exercising self-denial! I am determined, however, through the grace of God, to try again.

"Saturday, June 20th. On reading over my past diary, I find it is full of mourning and complaints. And I am still in the same case. O! what unfaithfulness, depravity, and sinfulness! Blind in my understanding! stubborn in my will! depraved in my affections! guilty in my conscience! condemned by my own judgment! shut up in my insensibility! What must I do? 'Lord, I am oppressed; undertake for me.' I feel a determination to try once more. O for power!"

At the Conference of 1815 it was appointed that the chairmen of districts should, at each district meeting, examine every preacher on trial respecting the course of theological reading which he had pursued during the preceding year; for which purpose, every such preacher was required to deliver to the chairman of his district a list of the books which he had read since the preceding district meeting. These lists were to be laid before the meeting, that the senior brethren might have an opportunity of giving to the junior preachers such advices and directions respecting their studies as might appear to be necessary. To this regulation Mr. Stoner conscientiously attended.[1] It appears that one year he presented a list of *forty-one* volumes,

---

1   The following is the list which he presented in 1817:
Wesley's Works, 16 vols.
Burnet on the Articles.
Homilies of the Church of England.
Newton on the Prophecies, 2 vols.
Neal's history of the Puritans, 2 vols.
Simpson's Plea for the Deity of Jesus.
Mather's Student and Preacher.
Burder's Oriental Customs, 2 vols.
Magee on Atonement and Sacrifice, 2 vols.
Watts's Works, 6 vols.
Collyer's Lectures on Miracles.
Ditto on Prophecies.

besides *eighty-one* on various subjects which he did not insert in his list. Another year he presented a list of *thirty-six,* exclusive of *fifty-seven* others. The lists which he prepared consisted generally of well-chosen theological works, and some of them large ones. This sufficiently proves his diligence, especially when it is remembered that he read with great attention, and that he was at the same time busily engaged with his compositions for the pulpit. It is remarkable that he has not mentioned any of the "advices and directions respecting his studies," which the senior preachers gave him during the successive years of his probation; but there can be no doubt that whatever he might receive of this kind he would carefully observe.

The period had now arrived when, according to the usages of the Wesleyan Connexion, he was to be publicly admitted into full ministerial union with that body. "The time is approaching," he remarks in his diary of April 28th, "when I must be admitted into full connexion. And it becomes me as an honest man, a Christian, and a minister, to give the subject the most deliberate consideration. O! let thy light shine!" He passed through the different examinations with much credit to himself; "witnessed a good confession" in the public congregation at Leeds "before many witnesses;" and took his place in the itinerancy with the cordial and unanimous approbation of his assembled brethren.

Immediately after Conference he entered into the marriage state with Miss Hannah Roberts, who has already been named as the first seal to his ministry at Holmfirth. The reasons for which he entered into this state, in addition to its being God's ordinance, were, as he remarks in his diary, "1. That he might have a help to 'growth in grace.' 2. That he might have a stimulus to study and diligence. 3. That he might have assistance against his natural timidity. 4. That he might have a counsellor and comforter in all his concerns. 5. That he might have an intimate friend to point out to him his faults, etc." In these things he was not disappointed. Mrs. Stoner proved a help

---

Dick on the Inspiration of Scripture.
Paley's Natural Theology, 2 vols.
Chalmers's Astronomical Discourses.
Ryan's History of the Effects of Religion on Mankind.

Ministry at Huddersfield

meet for him; and during the few years that their union was permitted to continue, it seems to have been eminently happy.

"Monday, November 23rd, 1818. I feel once again the drawings and quickenings of the Holy Spirit. Yesterday was a pretty good day. In the evening I had an opportunity of recommending religion to a gentleman who has just lost his pious partner, but was overcome by my natural timidity. Lord, forgive me, and grant me more courage!

"Tuesday, 24th. Glory be to my God, he is still drawing me to himself. In preaching last night, the fear of man made me tremble, a dissenting minister being present. My heart beat violently in repeating the Lord's prayer; but God helped me through, and with some degree of enlargement of heart. But what unfaithfulness! I think far more about getting through my work than about being useful to the people. In the band-meeting I felt wanderings of mind. Today I had a call to visit two sick people, but find a shameful reluctance to such duties.

"Thursday, 26th. Through want of private devotion, I felt my soul dead this morning; but God has again visited me. While writing on the conversation of Moses and Elijah with Christ, my heart was warmed! O may I

> Of nothing think or speak beside,
> My Lord, my Love, is crucified!

"June 12th, 1819. In the former part of this week my mind was revived. While meeting a class was softened, and tears of contrition and of gratitude plentifully flowed. My God, now take full possession of my heart!

"Friday, 25th. Praised be the name of my God that he still spares me. I am a sinner, but Christ has died for me! And here is my only confidence. My mind is much depressed and exercised. I feel a suggestion which would prompt me to leave the work of the ministry, for reasons something like the following: 1. My preaching seems to be nearly useless. It is very rarely that I have heard of any convictions or conversions of late. 2. Such is my excessive and hitherto unconquerable timidity and bashfulness, that I cannot fulfil the necessary duties of my office. 3. My increasing weakness of constitution. But I dare not desist. I *had* a call from God, I am convinced; and if that call is not now so clear, it is perhaps through my unfaithfulness. The first reason above-mentioned arises from my want of piety; the second, from my want of self-denial; and the third, partly from my injudicious method of speaking. I yet feel resolved to give myself to God. He is drawing me in some degree after himself. May he save me to the uttermost!

"Wednesday, 30th. My Lord, help me to attend continually to first principles. 'As ye have received Christ Jesus the Lord, so walk ye in him.' I endeavour to preach the Methodist doctrines as Mr. Wesley preached them, and to observe all the parts of our discipline. But I want more *love.* Come, Lord!"

From the account which Mr. Stoner has occasionally given of his want of ministerial success in the Huddersfield Circuit, it might be concluded that his "labour" while there was comparatively "in vain." Such a conclusion, however, would be manifestly incorrect. It ought to be considered that his solicitude for souls was incessant and extreme; that he could satisfy himself with nothing but visible and striking manifestations of divine power; and that when he adverted to this subject in his diary, he generally struggled with a painful degree of mental depression. Besides, according to the wise appointment of almighty God, it often happens that success, where it really exists, is mercifully concealed from those who have been chiefly instrumental in promoting it. "The bread cast upon the waters," however, is not lost, though it may not appear until "after many days." Facts incontestably prove that, in conjunction with his excellent colleagues, Mr. Stoner enjoyed a gratifying degree of official prosperity in Huddersfield and the neighbouring villages. During the three years that he spent there, *four hundred and ten* members were added to the societies. The increasing congregations at Huddersfield called also for the erection of the new chapel (the largest Methodist place of worship either in Great Britain or America, with the exception, perhaps, of the Brunswick chapel at Leeds), by which an opportunity was afforded of more widely extending the influence of religious instruction. From many of the friends he received encouraging proofs of affectionate attention, of which he was gratefully sensible. He particularly mentions the kindness of John Dyson, Esq., of Newhouse, with whom he resided a considerable time.

His religious experience during a part of this period will be thought often gloomy and occasionally desponding. Fully convinced as he now was of the necessity of a larger communication of sanctifying grace, it is not extraordinary that he became more keenly and painfully alive to the remaining corruptions of his nature. Like the exemplary Brainerd also, whom he resembled in many far more desirable qualities, there can be little doubt that he had, in his constitutional temperament, a strong tendency to melancholy and dejection.[1] To hear him complain of fickleness, indolence, and want of zeal may appear remarkable even to his most intimate friends, who know that he was almost proverbial for the opposite properties. By these disclosures of the secret exercises of his heart it will be discovered how those opposite properties were attained. He saw his failings; he guarded against them with assiduity and vigilance; and he sought those succours from above by which he so entirely overcame them. This is the course which others must pursue who would imitate his example and obtain similar triumphs. In the pursuit of Christian virtue, too much has sometimes been attributed to the ductility of nature; too little to the persevering efforts of spiritual discipline, accompanied by the indispensable supplies of divine grace. "None are *supinely* good." Prayer, watchfulness, self-denial, faith and perseverance are requisite; and to these, exercised in the strength of God, are promised the sublime victories and "undefiled rewards" of heavenly wisdom.

---

[1] David Brainerd (1718–1747), American missionary.

6

Ministry at Bradford

Extraordinary success of Mr. Stoner's ministry in the Bradford Circuit, to which he is next appointed—The spirit in which he entered upon his new station—Rev. Isaac Turton's testimony to his zeal and usefulness—Extracts from his diary—He publishes a sermon on occasion of the death of his Majesty, George III—Part of a letter to the Rev. John Hanwell—Other extracts from his diary and correspondence, particularly illustrative of his earnest pursuit of Christian holiness—Remarks on his progress in the attainment of it—Farther extracts from his diary and correspondence—Observations on his general habits while at Bradford, and especially on his entire conviction of the necessity of divine influence to any degree of ministerial success.

Christian ministers who, during the progress of life discharge the duties of their function in different situations, are sometimes favoured in certain places with peculiar and memorable success. To such places their talents and habits are, perhaps, particularly adapted; and in them they are honoured by the great Lord of all with larger and more abundant effusions of his hallowing influence. That illustrious pattern of ministerial zeal and fidelity, St. Paul, seems never to have been entirely unsuccessful. He could say, "Thanks be unto God, which *always* causeth us to triumph in Christ, and maketh manifest the savour of his knowledge by us *in every place*." Yet there were scenes in which even his success was more striking and observable: at Antioch, for example, at Philippi, at Thessalonica, at Ephesus—places which he ever remembered with feelings of grateful and affectionate delight. Ordinary teachers of divine truth still experience similar visitations. On reviewing the course of their public labours, they can dwell with singular pleasure on bright and flourishing periods of their own history; can recall to mind seasons in which they were more than usually instrumental in extending the triumphs of truth and mercy; and can look forward to that consummation of all things,

Ministry at Bradford

when they shall be permitted to present many, gathered from the more prosperous scenes of their earthly toil, who shall be their "joy and crown of rejoicing" in the day of the Lord Jesus.

To such a station of special and extensive success Mr. Stoner was providentially directed when, in the year 1819, he received an appointment to the Bradford Circuit. Here also he continued three years. He enjoyed the privilege of having for his superintendents, for the first year, the Rev. Isaac Turton, and for the remaining two, the Rev. Joseph Entwisle. This was undoubtedly the best portion of his useful life. In connexion with his excellent colleagues, he laboured assiduously in every part of his work, witnessed an uncommon manifestation of divine grace, and at the close of his term, in addition to other evidences of prosperity, could rejoice over a clear increase to the different societies of more than *one thousand souls*. His superintendents unite in testifying that he was eminently successful in the awakening and conversion of sinners. Nor was he merely beneficial to others. During this period, as will sufficiently appear from his diary, he made great personal progress in Christian attainments.

He entered upon the work of his new Circuit in an exemplary spirit. "Bradford, August 27th," he writes in his diary. "Yesterday we came to this place, not only by God's permission, but I trust also by his special appointment. I trust that the finger of God pointed to Bradford, and that he will afford his presence and blessing. On my entering into this new Circuit, I would dedicate myself afresh to God, and engage in a new course. Come, my Lord, and take full possession! I am resolved, *divino auxilio* 1. That I will rise earlier. 2. That I will spend two hours daily in searching the Scriptures, self-examination, meditation, prayer, keeping diary, etc. 3. That in those hours I will read a chapter of Hebrew and Greek alternately, every day. 4. That I will read to my wife a chapter of Dr. Clarke daily, and of Mr. Wesley's Works at least a little every day. '*Nulla dies sine linea.*' 5. That I will read the Bible regularly according to Holroyd,[1] part of it on my knees before God. 6. I will, I must spend more time in visiting the sick and poor. 7. I must make or remake a sermon every week, if possible; at least every fortnight. 8. I will continue to dedicate one

---

1 See "Tables for reading the Scriptures in one Year," by the Rev. J. B. Holroyd.

tenth of my income to God. 9. I will fast as often as I find it prudent. 10. I must do something by way of instructing the rising generation. 11. I must, I must be more spiritually-minded, especially in company. But I know that all these resolutions will be made in vain except God create my heart anew. I have been striving to give myself to God. But I want some token for good, some proof that I am the Lord's, and his messenger." The above resolutions clearly display the state of his mind in reference to himself and his work. He sometimes complains that he has not been able to observe them, and pronounces sentence upon himself with his usual severity: but the very formation of them proves how ardently he desired to "work out his own salvation" and to "make full proof of his ministry."

Of his general deportment and activity during the first year he spent at Bradford, Mr. Turton has favoured the writers with the following account: "When we first met, I thought him very shy and reserved, and had my doubts whether I should have a comfortable year with him as a colleague. But in a short time he became more free and communicative; and during the time we were together, we spent many a pleasant and profitable hour in conversation and prayer with each other. We laboured together in perfect harmony, and saw considerable fruit of our labours. During the winter quarter, we agreed to hold a watch-night in nearly every country place in the Circuit, hoping that this would be useful to the people generally and more especially to the societies. And so it proved, for in almost every place we afterwards heard that good was done. Our plan was this: We went together, accompanied by three or four pious, lively, and zealous prayer leaders and local preachers; and after a short sermon delivered in as pointed, powerful, and pithy a manner as possible, the brethren who went with us prayed, particularly for the people present and the inhabitants of the place. We generally had a much larger company than on ordinary occasions, and considerable interest was excited among the people. I commonly prevailed on Mr. Stoner to preach; and his word was indeed 'with power,' producing an immediate and visible effect, especially on strangers who had been induced to attend because a watch-night was to be held."

Other valuable communications from Mr. Turton and Mr. Entwisle will be more properly reserved for the last chapter in this work, which contains a description of Mr. Stoner's character.

"Thursday, September 9th," he writes, "Blessed be God, I have been enabled hitherto to keep most of my resolutions. But, after all, I often feel lifeless and indifferent. Lord, quicken me! I want to be useful. I cannot be satisfied that my call to Bradford is of God until I hear of some awakenings. Praise the Lord, I met the other day with a man who was awakened under an occasional sermon that I preached here a year or two ago. O Lord, revive Thy work!'

"Thursday, November 25th. Glory be to God for the continuance of his infinite mercy to my body and soul. When I consider my own sinfulness and the divine purity and majesty, I wonder that God spares me; and yet my heart is so hard and unfeeling that I am almost unaffected by it. I have partly attended to some of my resolutions, made when I came to this Circuit; but I am woefully deficient. My heart is full of pride and self-will and every evil. I waste much precious time in bed, in idle conversation, in unprofitable reading, etc. I do not visit the sick and poor as I ought to do. I do not preach for souls. My heart is *ice* when it ought to *be flame*. Lord, undertake for me! Nothing affects my heart so much as pious biography. I read this morning, *Memoirs of Mrs. Cooper.* How was I melted and ashamed! Nothing but the omnipotent grace of God can raise me out of this quagmire into which I am sunk. This grace is to be obtained only by prayer; yet when I attempt to pray, I feel such indifference, such wanderings, such listlessness! But 'I will arise, and go to my Father.'

"Saturday evening, December 4th. The impressions made on my mind by reading the memoir last week are not effaced. Blessed be God, I feel the savour of them still. I had a struggle to conquer one of my besetments, but I trust I am now the conqueror. I feel that Christ is mine. But I long to be cleansed from all sin. I feel at times that pride almost fills my heart. This evening, in drawing nigh to God, I enjoyed enlargement of soul, and had such a view of my danger and responsibility, that I was constrained to ask my God, if he saw I should dishonour his cause and lose my soul that he would *now* breathe his nature into my heart and take me home.

My constitutional besetment, timidity, yet conquers me. It keeps me from visiting the sick and poor, from speaking to all I meet with on spiritual subjects, from recommending the Saviour wherever I come, from making myself easy and accessible to all. I know I am wrong. It is my daily grief and burden, and yet I cannot conquer. Sometimes I am tempted to murmur that the Almighty has given me such a shrinking spirit and yet called me into a public station. Cowper's description of his timidity is a strong picture of mine, only a shade or two deeper. But cannot grace conquer all this? I do not know. I have been told that Mr. Bramwell, holy as he was, was on some occasions excessively timid. Lord, help me!"

On the 16th of February, 1820, he preached a sermon at Bradford on occasion of the death of his late majesty George III and was afterwards solicited to furnish a copy of it for publication. To this he reluctantly consented. His text was 1 Chron. 29:28: "And he died in a good old age, full of days, riches, and honour." The sermon is not without merit, but it by no means affords a correct specimen of Mr. Stoner's pulpit compositions. It consists chiefly of anecdotes illustrative of the revered monarch's character; but the character seems subservient to the anecdotes, rather than the anecdotes to the character. The reflections discover but little vigour and expansion of thought; and the diction, compared with Mr. Stoner's usual energy of style, is rather feeble. The publication appears, however, to have been useful at the time, particularly as unfolding the religious and moral excellencies of his late majesty, and testifying the unaffected sentiments of loyalty by which the Methodist Connexion have always wished to be distinguished.

In a letter to Mr. Hanwell, despatched on the 20th of March, he incidentally uses the word *impulses,* and adds, "This self-same word *impulses* which has just dropped from my pen brings before my mind many unpleasant ideas. By *impulses,* by fits and starts I mean, I have studied, I have prayed, I have preached, I have done everything. Had I been governed by one regular propensity of diligence, as you appear always to be, I should have been saved from many evils which arise from being propelled so irregularly by *impulses.* God forgive me! Time is rolling away. How soon will life be gone, and how careless and sleepy and indolent am I! Our growth in grace and our enjoyment of the consolations of religion depend, under God, on our own diligence. 'The diligent soul shall be made fat.' 'The diligent hand maketh rich.' May God help me! In those seasons when you have power with God, remember me; and you will not be forgotten in the feeble prayers of your affectionate friend."

"Saturday, June 3rd," he remarks in his diary, "Three weeks ago God quickened my soul. I felt the drawings of his Spirit and was enabled to run after him. For several days I enjoyed a considerable degree of communion with him. But since then, I have attended the district meeting, and have been several times from home. In consequence of this, my seasons of devotion have not been so regular. This has intercepted my intercourse with the Saviour and brought deadness into my soul. This evening I feel resolved, by God's help, to start again. I want to be more diligent in redeeming time, more assiduous in visiting the sick and poor, more earnest in winning souls to Christ, and to enjoy uninterrupted communion with God. I see more into the advantage and duty of communion with God. 'My soul, wait thou upon God.' Send up every moment thy prayers and praises and expect, in return, the communications of grace. This would keep me in peace. This would save me from many temptations. This would help me over my besetments. This would make my whole life a sacrifice. 'My God, give me this communion with thyself!'

"Wednesday, 7th. The reading of Mr. Bramwell's life has been much, very much, blessed to my soul. I am humbled, quickened, ashamed, and encouraged. My soul is going out after God. There is nothing in earth or heaven that I desire so much as a clean heart. Yesterday I spent a considerable time in prayer, in wrestling prayer; but I could not lay hold. I have been struggling again this morning, but something keeps me back. My heart feels hard. Something whispers that I am seeking the blessing from a wrong motive, even from pride—that I want to be holy only that I may be more zealous and more useful and therefore more popular. This surely is from the devil; surely it is impossible to seek after a clean heart from such a motive. I am fully certain that if such be my motive, I shall never obtain. But I can appeal to the searcher of hearts that, as far as I know myself, I desire to be swayed by no other motive than his glory. What then is it that keeps me from the blessing? I think I am willing to give all up, to 'sell all, that I may secure this pearl of great price.' But am I seeking it by the *works of the law?* I hope not. I know it must be by *faith*, and through the *blood of Christ* alone. Could I pray for a thousand years, could I weep tears of blood, could I 'give all my goods to feed the poor, and my body to be burned'—all this is nothing as to the deserving of salvation. It is salvation by *faith*. But what is this *faith?* What am I to believe? I do believe that Christ is *able* to save me. I believe that he is willing to save me. I believe that he is able and willing to save me *now*. Yea, I believe that he *will* save me, if I be faithful to the grace of God. But all this does not bring the blessing. I want to believe myself into the possession of it. It is my part to believe—by a naked faith to hang on a naked Christ. It is God's part to bless. He knows how and when to do it. Let me attend to my duty and leave God's part to his own wisdom. Blessed then, or unblessed, here I will stay. I believe—Lord, help me against my unbelief. Through the grace of God I will not give up the contest. I bless God, I enjoy already more power with him. I feel the intercourse open. I was enabled to take up my cross yesterday by going to see the sick and poor. I felt the power of God last night at Daisy Hill. I want, above all things, to be emptied of sin and filled with God.

"Thursday, 8th. Praise the Lord, O my soul! I have been again wrestling this morning for an hour with my Saviour for a clean heart. I felt restless and eager to obtain the blessing. God gave me this promise, on which I desire to lean, Zeph. 3:14-15: 'Sing, O daughter of Zion; shout, O Israel; be glad and rejoice with all the heart, O daughter of Jerusalem. The Lord hath taken away thy judgments, he hath cast out thine enemy: the King of Israel, even the Lord, is in the midst of thee: thou shalt not see evil any more.' I feel an increased degree of confidence, but I want the witness of my full sanctification. Mr. Wesley speaks of the clear witness of this blessing as well as of the forgiveness of sin. This is what I desire. I felt this morning a degree of impatience because the Lord does not come as soon as I ask him. I think this is wrong. I ought to be, as the poet has it, *'restless, resigned.'* I desire this *restlessness* and yet this *resignation*. Yesterday

I was generally kept by the power of God. My communion with him was pretty regular. I was enabled to be tolerably diligent, and to take up my cross in visiting the sick. Praise the Lord! But yet how immensely far am I from the mark!

"Friday, 9th. I feel it is as necessary to be as earnest, as watchful, as wrestling, and as prayerful to *keep* grace as to *get* it. Yesterday I did not obey the 'still small voice' of the Spirit which called me to prayer; and I felt a degree of coldness creep on, with the rising of an evil temper. In the evening, I had little liberty in preaching, except in the application, when I felt a concern for the souls of my hearers. This morning I had a violent onset. Something suggested that holiness was not worth the price I had to pay for it—this self-denial, this taking up the cross, this wrestling in prayer, this rising in a morning, this redeeming the time as it flies, this determined opposition and struggle against every evil thought as it rises. But, thank God, through his grace I conquered. Yet while I strove to wrestle for an hour with him, it was to me too much as a 'dry breast.' Praise the Lord for another promise: 'Thine iniquity is taken away, and thy sin purged.' I engaged that, if the Lord would give me a promise, I would believe it. He has given me this encouraging declaration, and I am bound to believe it. Lord, I do believe it. But I want the seal, the witness. I want not only the 'iniquity to be taken away,' but my soul to be 'filled with the fulness of God.' Lord, fill me!

"Saturday, 10th. Praise the Lord, my mind is at peace, stayed upon God. Yesterday I enjoyed communion with God without much interruption. I was enabled to take up my cross and redeem the time. I felt the presence of the Lord last night at Horton. This morning I have again been pleading with God for an hour for all his fulness. I again feel the application of the word, 'Thine iniquity is taken away, and thy sin purged.' My soul labours to believe it. I have given all up to God. There is nothing I want to keep for myself, the world, or the devil. I have given God all. And, through Christ, claim all. I take Christ as my 'all in all;' and here my soul rests. He will never condemn me for believing too boldly, if I only labour with all my soul to obtain that for which I believe. I do not yet feel the transporting raptures I expect—the sealing of the Spirit—the indubitable witness of my full sanctification—but I do feel that I can lie in the dust, and simply say, 'Speak, Lord; for thy servant heareth.'

> To know thou tak'st me for thine own,
> O what a happiness is this!

"Sunday, 11th. Glory be to God, I yet experience his power and love. I went to the band-meeting last night expecting to receive the blessing, but I did not. I have been wrestling with God for it this morning, but I cannot lay hold. Lord, show me the hindrance. What can it be? I cannot discover it. I feel that ceaseless resolution, prayer, and watchfulness are necessary to my advancing in the divine life. I was unwatchful for some time yesterday, and it brought a degree of darkness into my soul. I want to live in the spirit of self-denial, self-mortification, and taking up the cross.

> All that to the end endure
> The cross, shall wear the crown.

"Monday, 12th. I thank my God for the comforts I enjoyed yesterday. In the morning I had a good season, and in the afternoon a considerable degree of liberty of speech. I feel an earnest desire that souls may be saved. I yet am thirsting for a clean heart. Yesterday I discovered several things which are inconsistent with a clean heart. 1. I felt, for two or three moments at different times, the indulgence of evil thoughts. 2. I found pride lurking within me, suggesting that I had preached well, etc. By proposing to myself a few questions this morning, I detected the pride of my heart. 'Am I as willing that, when souls are saved under my ministry, the instrument should be unknown as that it should be published? Am I as willing that souls should be saved under any other minister as myself? Am I as thankful when souls are saved by other means as when they are saved under my preaching?' These questions, pushed home, disclosed my pride. 3. I felt a reluctance, which I did not always conquer, to reprove sin, Sabbath-breaking, etc. 4. I feel within a sort of reluctance and indifference to the duty of prayer. Lord, help me! I know if the devil can only get me to lay aside prayer, all is over. Come, my Lord, and take my heart. I want pride destroying. I want to be nothing; to be clothed with humility; to be swallowed up of love. 'Lord, I am thine: save me!'

"Tuesday, 13th. Lord, what shall I do to obtain this perfect love? Christ is able and willing to give the blessing now. The hindrance, therefore, must be all in me. But how is it? I feel my need of this blessing. I have a restless desire after it. I strive to seek it with all my heart. So far as I know myself, I am willing to part with everything to obtain it. I seek it through the blood of Christ, and I strive to seek by faith. I believe, as far as I know, as well as I can; and yet I cannot struggle into this perfect love. Come, Lord Jesus, take my heart! Lord, if there be anything in my heart or life that prevents me from receiving the blessing, show it me, and remove it. Yesterday, I had a pretty good day on the whole. In preaching here last night I enjoyed tolerable liberty. Praise the Lord, O my soul!

"Wednesday, 14th. Glory be to God, I feel that I am the Lord's. I have been giving myself again to my Saviour and my Lord. I love my Saviour. I feel his love in my heart. I can say with confidence, 'Lord, thou knowest all things; thou knowest that I love thee.' 'Whom have I in heaven but thee? and there is none upon earth that I desire beside thee.' While wrestling this morning with God for a clean heart, I felt much nearness to him—much of his presence. I thought myself not far from the kingdom of God, but I could not step in. I want the power of faith, and I want to know how to use it. Unbelief is the accursed bar. So far as I know, I am willing, through God's grace, to give up all; to do or suffer anything; to be used for God or to be laid aside for God; to be exalted for God or to be trampled on for God; so that he would fill me with his perfect love! Lord, I would still look up. I would be still expecting the descent of the Holy Ghost. Come, and fill my heart! The Lord has now kept me for a week. Satan tells me that this will soon be over; that, according to my usual instability, this fit of earnestness will speedily be spent; but he who has kept me a week can keep me a month or a year. The present moment is mine. Lord, help me to use it aright!

"Thursday, 15th. This morning I have had a hard struggle. Three quarters of an hour I waited at God's feet. I could not lay hold. I could not get my mind fixed. Wandering thoughts would break in. It seemed to be the 'hour and power of darkness.' But by struggling on and calling to the strong for strength, I obtained at length a degree of liberty. Yesterday afternoon I felt a deadness, and shyness, and coldness creeping over my soul. I prayed two or three times and found no help. My mind became somewhat alarmed lest I should be sinking into my former state of indifference. I went again to God and at last found liberty of soul and ease of access. I feel in danger, great danger. I do not watch sufficiently. I want continually to walk with God; to do everything in the name of my Lord Jesus Christ; to speak, and think, and read, and eat, and walk, and pray, and preach; in a word, to do all to the glory of God. Lord, save me!

"Friday, 16th. Glory be to God for his sparing and saving mercy. Yesterday I felt a considerable degree of coldness. I am not so watchful as I have been. I indulged wandering thoughts. I did not hold constant communion with God. I was fast sinking; but, blessed be God, I feel my desires and resolutions kindled afresh. God save me! Lord, save me now! A thought occurred to my mind this morning that the reason why I did not obtain the second blessing was that I was not clear in the enjoyment of the first. I examined myself. I feel that I am a sinner, that Christ died for sinners, that he died for me; and here is my sole reliance. Lord, I am condemned, but Christ has died. I feel that I am his and he is mine. I opened to a passage which instructs and encourages: 'I wait for the Lord, my soul doth wait, and in his word do I hope. My soul waiteth for the Lord more than they that watch for the morning. Let Israel hope in the Lord: for with the Lord there is mercy, and with him is plenteous redemption. And he shall redeem Israel from all his iniquities.' O my God, accomplish such promises in my soul!

"Saturday, 17th. Glory be to God, I still feel his saving power. I feel that I believe in Christ. I am afraid that I am not thankful enough for the ten thousand mercies that I receive. The Lord still enables me to spend no more than six hours in bed; to devote an hour to prayer in the morning, and to take up the cross in going to see the sick; and generally through the day to hold communion with him. But I want the fulness—perfect humility, perfect patience, perfect love. My union with God is often interrupted. The devil eagerly strives to reduce me to my former state of indifference. I was powerfully beset with temptations this morning; but, blessed be God, he does deliver

Ministry at Bradford 85

and he will deliver. May he fill me with his fulness! I want to do everything in the name of Jesus.

"Sunday, 18th. My soul is still athirst for God. Last night, at the band-meeting, I seemed to be just on the verge of receiving the blessing; but I could not struggle through. Again this morning I have been pleading for it, but I cannot get hold of it. Lord, what is the hindrance? Am I not in *sufficient earnest?* Am I not seeking the blessing with all my heart? Yes, Lord, as far as I know my heart, I am. So far as I can judge, my whole soul is engaged. Is there anything that I have not given up? I do not know that there is. Everything that I know of, I am willing to sacrifice. I feel willing, through the grace of God, to be anything or nothing so that I can but enter into this rest. Am I seeking the blessing by the *law of works?* I hope not, but I fear there is too much dependence on my own seeking and doings. Lord, remove this prop. Am I seeking it by *faith?* I know it can be obtained only by faith. And it is by faith that I wish to seek it. Lord, help me to believe!

"Monday, 10th. Glory be to God, I enjoyed his presence and help yesterday. I had three good times at the chapel. Whilst I was preaching a funeral sermon, my heart was softened. This morning, while striving to wrestle with God, I was much troubled with wandering thoughts; but towards the close of the hour I felt greater liberty. I do not yet receive the blessing. I am much afraid of sinking down into a state of indifference if I do not get it soon. Lord, come to my help! I want to feel that *I* am nothing, that *great I* is entirely annihilated, and that Christ is all in all! O for a struggle into God!

"Tuesday, 20th. This morning, while I have been engaged in prayer, I have felt greater earnestness, greater resolution and stronger faith, I think, than I ever felt. I seemed to myself just on the threshold of salvation. O that I could enter in! God gave me this passage, 'Many waters cannot quench love, neither can the floods drown it: if a man would give all the substance of his house for love, it would utterly be contemned.' From this passage I thought I discovered that I was making a sort of bargain with God, that if he would sell me his perfect love, I would sell him all I have and am as a sort of equivalent for it; but I see this is not the way. I am to give all up, but this is nothing as to the meriting of salvation. I am to receive it purely through the merits of Christ. O that I knew how to believe!

"Wednesday, 21st. 'Speak, Lord; for thy servant heareth.' This is the present feeling of my soul. I feel willing to relinquish all, and through Christ to receive salvation as the free gift of God. Last night, at Heaton, I felt my heart drawn out for the sinners of that place. O my God, heal them!

"Friday, 23rd. Yesterday morning I rose too late; but still I spent my hour in prayer, and enjoyed much nearness to God whilst I was praying. I felt willing to surrender all and to receive salvation as the free gift of God in Christ Jesus. But through the day I suffered my heart to grow languid and to wander, so that last night, at Parsley, I felt but little power. When I came to my duty this morning, I had a mighty contest. My heart was hard, and reluctant, and indifferent. I felt a distance between God and my soul. The devil perplexed me much with wandering thoughts; but at length I wrestled and prayed till I obtained deliverance. The door of access was again set open; the channel of intercourse was renewed, and I felt power with God. I still search for a clean heart, and sometimes to myself seem very near it; but I cannot get hold. I feel desirous above all things to receive it. Christ I know is desirous above all things to give it. Then how is it that I cannot lay hold? What is it that hinders? So far as God has given me light, I am willing to give up all. I strive to seek it with my whole soul, and to seek it by faith. Lord, have mercy upon me, and teach me the way, that I may walk in it!

"Saturday, 24th. My heart is hard. I thank God, however, that I am enabled in a great degree to deny myself, to take up my cross, to follow him in the way of duty, to live more in the spirit of prayer than I used to do, and to be earnest in my application to him for a clean heart; but still I do not receive the blessing. My soul is discouraged and disheartened. Lord, help me to be more in earnest, and direct me in the way of faith!

"Monday, 26th. Glory, glory be to God! This morning, while I have been praying, he has blessed me. My heart is watered, softened, and quickened. I feel a stronger confidence than ever that from sin and death and hell God will redeem my soul. Yesterday, in the afternoon, I had a specially good season. But I want filling with God.

"Wednesday, 28th. On looking over the two past days, I see much reason for humility and much for praise. On Monday, in our quarterly meeting, etc., all was peace. At our watch-night we had a blessed season. Last night at Frizingley the power of the Lord was present to heal. Yesterday morning, I felt considerable power to plead with God. But during the day I was off my guard. I was unwatchful. I got into a light spirit. I did not pray as I ought. However, I thank God, I have enjoyed a degree of liberty in again coming to him. I feel it profitable to read a chapter or two on my knees and to pray over them. The prayer in Eph. 3:14, etc., 'For this cause I bow my knees,' etc., appears to contain an infinite fulness. O that I could enter in!

"Thursday, 20th. I feel my soul still resolved. Last night at Low Moor I had a good time. I pray for a clean heart, but I do not receive; and I cannot discover the reason, except perhaps it is that I am not equally earnest throughout the day. I have been reading Fuller's *Life of Pearce*, and have been much benefited by it.[1] O that I could imitate his earnestness, his humility, his affection!

"Friday, 30th. Yesterday my heart wandered again too much. I was at Wibsey, but had little feeling and little faith. I have set apart this day for fasting and prayer. I have been earnestly praying to be filled with the Spirit, and have been renewing my covenant with God according to Alleine's form, and feel willing to give up all and to become the entire servant of the Lord. I, David Stoner, a wicked sinner, a child of ten thousand mercies, do promise, through God's grace, from this hour to devote myself and my whole life to his glory through his Son. In testimony of which, I hereto, in the presence of God and of his holy angels, solemnly subscribe my hand. DAVID STONER."

About this time he wrote to Mr. Hanwell: "We have an excellent band-meeting on Saturday evenings in our vestry, at which we have several clear witnesses of the power of Christ to cleanse from all sin. These testimonies, as well as the life that is among our people generally, and the conversions which we see, rejoice my heart, inasmuch as

---

1   Andrew Fuller, *Memoir of Rev. Samuel Pearce Who was United with Carey and Others in Establishing Missions in India, 1793. With Additions from his Son, Rev. W. H. Pearce, Missionary at Calcutta*. (American Tract Society c.1810)

they are proofs that the glory is not departed from us and that God has not forsaken us. I have lately read the *Life of Socinus* by Toulmin. I entered upon it with caution, lest I should be caught by the seducing words of man's wisdom and led from the truth. But I do not recollect that I ever read any work which more fully confirmed me in the Christian scheme. Such shuffling, and quibbling, and twisting, and racking, and torturing, to bend the Scriptures to a system, I never saw. I really do not conceive how any man of sense can believe that scheme cordially, except he be first given up to the delusion of the devil to believe a lie; and when a man is so given up, it seems, from experience, that he can swallow any absurdity. What do you think of Bramwell's *Life*?[1] When I read it, I was pleasingly disappointed. I was afraid there would be a great deal of captious querulousness in it, but there is very little. He was truly a great man of God. My soul was ashamed, humbled, and quickened in reading it. I do not know that the reading of any book ever produced such an effect upon my mind. You are acquainted in a very small degree with my fickleness. You know that I have resolved and re-resolved thousands of times that I would live nearer to God. But alas! my resolutions never lasted above a few days or a few weeks at the longest. The reading of Mr. B.'s Life has led me to begin again. My resolution has now lasted three weeks, and I still feel the force of it. I think I have got upon a better system than I ever did. Perseverance will do everything."

"Sunday, July 2nd. This morning I have been renewing my covenant with God. I give myself fully up to him. I take him as my God. I call him mine; I consider myself as his. I will 'reckon myself to be dead indeed unto sin.' I feel a settled confidence in God. I taste the peace of God. I hope he will be with me this day. I want to be filled with the Spirit. I have missed it, after I have prayed, in not 'watching thereunto with all perseverance and supplication for all saints.' Lord, help me to live this moment for Thee!

"Monday, 3rd. Rose this morning at four. Spent an hour on my knees. Felt much harassed with wandering thoughts. The devil hates prayer. Had a pretty good day yesterday. But I want to feel more

---

1   The second volume of Mr. Bramwell's *Memoirs* was not published when Mr. Stoner wrote the above. It is to the first volume, therefore, that his remarks are intended to apply.

restless and anxious about the conversion of sinners. Of what use is it preaching except good is done? Glory be to God, I heard of an instance on Saturday evening of a sinner being awakened under a sermon from, 'Behold, I stand at the door, and knock,' etc. Lord, make me more faithful!

"Tuesday, 4th. Yesterday I grieved the Spirit by not going out to visit the sick and poor. I indulged my indolence, having not had sufficient sleep the night before, and remained at home. But blessed be God, he again visited my soul at the chapel in the evening. While Mr. Turton was recommending the example of Christ, my heart was softened, and I was again determined to pursue the mind of Christ. This morning I have felt it good to draw near to God. My soul is enlivened. These words in the morning lesson I was enabled to plead and rely upon: 'The eternal God is thy refuge, and underneath are the everlasting arms: and he shall thrust out the enemy from before thee; and shall say, Destroy them.' I feel that God is my refuge, that his arms are underneath me to protect and support, and that he will thrust out and destroy my inward enemies. Lord, by thy strength I drag out this pride—now kill it; this unbelief—now destroy it; this self-will—now abolish it; this love of the world—now banish it! O that my soul were filled with God!

"Wednesday, 5th. Yesterday was a good day to my soul. God helped me to take up the cross and to visit the sick and poor. In reading Mr. Vasey's *Life*, I felt softened and quickened. We have held our first five-o'clock prayer-meeting this morning. The power of the Lord was present to heal. I do not yet clearly apprehend this full salvation. Sometimes I am ready to think I have it, and that I do not sufficiently distinguish between temptations and evil tempers. Lord, give me light and power!

"Thursday, 6th. The intercourse has again been opened this morning. Yesterday I neglected to take up a cross. My heart indulged some wanderings. I was not watchful and prayerful. Darkness and shyness got in. 'But, blessed be God for a throne of grace,' and for grace to come to it. Satan laboured hard this morning, by injecting wandering thoughts, to keep me at a distance. He hates prayer. I more than ever feel the necessity of it. Whilst I can continue to devote an hour every morning to this work, I think God will keep and help me. O for preserving grace!

> Keep me, keep me, gracious Lord;
> And never let me go.

"Friday, 7th. This morning I have again enjoyed nearness to God. I feel fully willing, as far as I know myself, to be the Lord's on the Lord's own terms. I sometimes think my heart is already cleansed, but I lose it by my refusing to acknowledge and believe it and by unwatchfulness. Now, at this moment, I do not know that I have anything, or feel anything, contrary to love. I should like to reckon myself *now* 'dead to sin' and filled with perfect love; but I am afraid of presuming, of reckoning without my host. O for the sealing power! O for the fulness of love! If my Saviour would come and fill one unutterably full of glory and of God, then I think I should be satisfied. But is not this to say, If Christ will save me first, I will then believe? Lord, teach me how to believe! and O keep me this day! I am going to the school committee at the Grove. Keep my thoughts, and tempers, and tongue, and actions! I want to pray without ceasing and to watch unto all perseverance, etc.

"Saturday, 8th. Blessed be God, my soul is alive. God said to me this morning while praying, 'Will, be thou clean?' Faith says, I am clean! But I want the fulness! Lord, save me!

"Sunday, 16th. This last week I have been from home on a visit to my friends at Barwick. Blessed be God this visit has not been in vain. I preached there on Wednesday evening and the word was not fruitless. All the glory be to God! I myself did not feel much. I was rather cramped than otherwise. But it seems, from what was said afterwards, that the word went home to several hearts. On Friday evening at the class one person said the word entered her heart like a two-edged sword. That evening, before the class was dismissed, she found liberty. During the first prayer at the class-meeting, I felt the power of God come down. My heart began to melt. While I was praying, I felt as if I was going to plunge into the fountain; but just at the moment something within me shrunk back and I did not then enter in. Through the meeting, I continued to wait on God;

and in praying again at the conclusion, I seemed to be within a hair's breadth of salvation. My heart softened, and warmed, and filled; my prayer was turned into praises and I could do nothing but shout, 'Glory be to God!' I felt that God had taken possession of my heart. This morning I enjoy in part the sweetness of it. I have been severely harassed with the idea that it was only enthusiasm or a delusion. But I wish to keep my evidence. I feel nothing contrary to love. I want to be every moment filled with God. Whether I hold or not, I am sure that God took full possession of my heart on the 14th of July."

That period of Mr. Stoner's life to which the preceding extracts have conducted us is very important in the history of his religious experience. One of the compilers of these pages was present at the class-meeting mentioned above. It was a memorable opportunity, a season of uncommon "refreshing from the presence of the Lord." Mr. Stoner was exceedingly earnest, and in the peculiar ardour of his desires after spiritual blessings appeared equally to forget the concerns of earth and the frailties of his own mortal nature. The writer distinctly remembers that part of the meeting when, in the vehemence of believing prayer he exclaimed, "My God, I am within a hair's breadth!" At that moment the penitent who had been convinced of sin on the Wednesday evening found peace; and shortly afterwards, Mr. Stoner received the blessing which he has recorded in terms so explicit and satisfactory. From his private papers, indeed, it appears that he did not always enjoy a clear and undisputed evidence of it. His views of the purity and extent of the divine law were exceedingly deep, and his conviction of the heights of holiness to which a man may be raised by the blood and Spirit of Christ unusually elevated. These, associated with his timid and scrupulous temper, sometimes gave advantage to his spiritual enemies and tended to obscure his evidence and impair his enjoyments. At such times, however, nothing could satisfy him but a renewed attestation of God's sanctifying grace to his heart. In his diary he often indulges in his wonted complaints, but he invariably expresses his determinate purpose to persevere in his high and heavenly pursuits.

On those extracts from his papers which have occupied several preceding pages it may not be superfluous to remark that they exhibit a sublime example of sincere and fervent piety. Designed as the simple effusions of his feelings and desires at the moment when he wrote, they differ widely from the language, too often, it is feared, unexamined and unfelt, of commonplace devotion, and afford a powerful representation of the lofty tendencies of the soul in pursuit of the highest good. To the lamentable apathy of many worldly philosophers such things may appear enthusiastic and absurd; but to the correct and enlarged views of superior intelligences it is doubtless matter of wonder and delight to see an immortal spirit, even while it tenants a house of clay, despising all the seductions of earth and sin, directing the full tide of its desires towards the incomprehensible and eternal God, and striving to lose itself in the unutterable plenitude of his love. Compared with the exalted aims of such a spirit, the toils of avarice, the blandishments of pleasure, and the projects of ambition dwindle into paltry insignificance and only attest the awful degradation of powers capable of infinitely nobler and more satisfying objects.

From this time the public labours of Mr. Stoner were crowned with more visible and extensive success. Holiness is the best preparation for usefulness. Such indeed is the regard which the Most High has for his own truth that he sometimes prospers it even when uttered by unhallowed lips; and such is his condescension that he often succeeds the endeavours of his servants who justly lament their own deficiencies and infirmities. The more, however, a minister of the sanctuary advances in personal purity, the more successful he generally becomes. Christian instruction ministered by him possesses a strong and commanding authority; it is sustained by a full conviction of its reality and recommended by the penetrating energy of personal and vital experience. To such a minister also God is commonly pleased to impart a larger portion of that assisting Spirit whose presence he seeks and on whose agency he humbly relies. This was verified in Mr. Stoner. On his return to Bradford, his friends observed that his sermons were, if possible, still more pointed and powerful—that they abounded more with fervent ejaculations for an immediate blessing—and that they were more eminently and evidently successful in the conversion of sinners and the edification of Christian believers.

"Friday, July 21st," he proceeds in his diary: "I have been again from home on a visit to Holmfirth and Lindley preaching a funeral sermon for my old friend, Betty Smith. But I have suffered loss in this journey and am much shorn of strength. Yet I feel resolved to begin again and to return to my former rules. While wrestling in prayer this morning my soul feels quickened. Lord, save me this day!

"Saturday, 22nd. I feel at liberty this morning. My mind is quickened. But I want the fulness. Speak, Lord, thy servant heareth!'

"Monday, 24th. Glory be to God for his assistance yesterday. We had a good love-feast at Low Moor, and last night at Heaton I felt much liberty. It distresses my heart that so little good is done. Another year is nearly gone, and O! how few sinners have been awakened under my ministry! Lord, if I am not in my right place and work, if my commission is run out, only show me, and I will not stay another day. But if it is thy will that I should still preach the gospel, O render it successful!

"Sunday, 30th. Glory be to God, last night and this morning my soul was revived. While praying, I have had near access to God. My desires are stronger; my confidence is stronger. May God be with me this day! I have presented the Lord my heart! He says, 'My son, give me thy heart.' I answered, 'My heart I give to thee.' I made the offer, and there I left it. O that the Almighty would accept it!

"Wednesday, August 2nd. I feel, blessed be God, that I am recovering the strength I had some time ago. On Sunday I had, upon the whole, a good day. At intervals since, I have enjoyed the presence of my God. But I do not yet live as I ought. I feel earnest in a morning during my hour's devotions, but I lose it again in the day. I do not live sufficiently in the spirit of prayer; and therefore, being unwatchful, I get shorn of my strength. Lord, keep me this day! I had a good time at the five o'clock meeting.

"Tuesday, 8th. My heart is still engaged with God for my own salvation and for the salvation of others. But I still have to mourn. I am not continually watchful. I am not always recollected. I often lose sight for a time of spiritual things. I feel, I think, more concern for the salvation of souls and the prosperity of Zion. I feel a spirit of prayer for Mr. Entwisle, who is expected at Bradford next year, that God will make him an abundant blessing to us all. Lord, if thou canst not make use of me, at least use him for thy glory; and let the next year be the best this Circuit ever saw!

"Saturday, 12th. Glory be to God for his continued mercy. I feel at this moment that I have hold of my Saviour. While I have been pleading with him, I have felt my heart considerably softened. I want humility above all things. I want to be willing to be anything or nothing! I see such desirableness in humility, I think, as I never did.

"Tuesday, 15th. When I examine myself impartially, I find that I am not so much in earnest as I was a few weeks since. To decrease in earnestness is the road to *lukewarmness, death,* and *ruin.* O Lord, quicken my soul! Still I am resolved, through the grace of God, to be his entirely and for ever.

"Wednesday, 16th. My soul is quickened. I feel stronger desires after the salvation of sinners. At Heaton last night my soul enjoyed the presence of God. I long to be filled with God. I heard yesterday good news from Barwick, that God is saving sinners. Lord, ride on!

"Thursday, 17th. I feel my heart drawn out this morning. I love my God. I believe in Christ. He is my Saviour. Preaching out of doors at White Abbey last night I felt blessed. Revive thy work, thou God of love!

"Monday, 21st. On Saturday evening I had a good time at the band. But at the close of the meeting I lost it all. A man came to request me to visit a sick woman. It was late. The house was at some distance. I was hot. The night was cold, etc., etc. I listened to flesh and blood and said 'No.' But I have been properly whipped for this since. It spoiled my day yesterday, but this morning I have again got the intercourse open. I thank God, this circumstance has convinced me that my conscience is increasingly tender.

"Sunday, 27th. My soul is alive! God is reviving his work among us! Glory be to him! My unworthy labours he is pleased to own. I feel a greater hatred to pride, a greater power over vain-glorious thoughts. May God save me this day!

"Tuesday, 29th. I am encouraged to hope that God is about to revive his work. Last night we had a good time at Brownroyd. My soul longs for the prosperity of Zion."

To Mr. Hanwell he writes, under the date of the last extract: "The thought of writing to you brings to my mind an association of ideas tinged with pleasing melancholy. 'Busy meddling memory,' in swift succession, musters up the past endearments of delicious hours spent in all the delights of friendship:

> Friendship! Mysterious cement of the soul,
> Sweet'ner of life, and solder of society!
> I owe thee much.

But to come down to plain prose, as I am no poet: the recollection of past scenes and past hours spent at Huddersfield fills my mind with pain and pleasure; and this mingled feeling now possesses my heart while I sit down to write to you. I have preached out of doors several times of late, and intend to do so whenever I have an opportunity. I find it also very useful to hold prayer-meetings, after preaching, in the country places. I have just been conversing with one of our good women on sanctification. She once enjoyed it but has now lost it. When I consider my privileges, my obligations, and my lukewarmness, I am ashamed before God. But yet I have cause for thankfulness. I can say it to the honour of God's grace, I never enjoyed so much of the power of religion these many years as I have done since I read Mr. Bramwell's *Life*. But again, if there is such a thing as perfect love to be enjoyed, why am I so foolish as to live without it? In the enjoyment of such a blessing I should be able to discharge all the awful duties of my office with much greater ease, comfort, steadiness and success. I wish to give the matter a fair trial. If I find the blessing unattainable, untenable, or inconsistent with my situation, I can but, at last, give it up. O pray for me that I may be 'filled with all the fulness of God.'"

"Tuesday, September 12th. Self-examination, I find, has been profitable. How is it with me now? I sometimes feel a disposition to be angry, peevish, and impatient. I feel pleasure in human applause, pain at human censure. I often feel a great reluctance to pray in private. I always feel a reluctance to visit the sick and poor. I find it exceedingly difficult to reprove sin and, on some occasions, to own my Master. I often feel wandering thoughts and unwatchfulness. I indulge in unprofitable speculations and useless conversations. I feel pride often rising in the pulpit. I am much wanting in spiritual-mindedness. I often feel the risings of envy and uncharitableness. I am much pestered with wandering thoughts in my private devotions. I am often ensnared with evil-speaking and slandering. Now who can think, after all this list of evils, that I am a Christian? O! how easy it is to wear a mask of Christianity and how difficult to have the heart right with God! However, thanks to God, I feel a confidence in Jesus as my Saviour. I feel, so far as I know myself, that it is the strongest desire of my heart to be fully sanctified. But O! what is it that hinders me from receiving this second blessing? I am ashamed of myself! So many of our people living in the enjoyment of it; I preaching it to others, urging others to seek it and professing to seek it myself, and yet living below it. Lord, what is it that hinders? I think, if Mr. Bramwell were somewhere within fifty miles, I would go to him that he might teach me and pray for me. But how foolish is this! Christ is here! with me and in me! Why then do I not enter into the promised land? Lord, I beseech thee remove the hindrance out of the way!

"Monday, 18th. My God hears and answers prayer. He has begun to revive his work. At Bowling he is saving sinners. O may the fire spread throughout the Circuit! On the whole, I had a good day yesterday at Horton. But yet I do not receive the fulness. Lord, help me!

"Monday, 25th. Glory be to God! My soul is happy in his love. Yesterday morning in my private devotions I gave myself up to him and felt nearness of access to him. In the former part of the love-feast in the afternoon I felt my soul filled and blessed. While a young woman was giving a clear statement of justification and sanctification, my soul was blessed indeed. In the latter part of the service my mind was dissipated. Several were crying out for mercy, which created much apparent confusion in the chapel. My condition was like that of a pilot in the midst of a storm when the vessel will not obey the helm. Glory be to God, however, the work is broken out, and I trust it will go forward. Last night, in preaching, I had a good time. And this morning my soul has been happy indeed. I feel that Christ has my heart. Whether this be sanctification or not, I have not the clear assurance; but my soul is full of love and joy. Lord, keep me!

"Friday, 29th. My heart is given up to God. So far as I know myself, I reserve nothing. Glory be to his name, I feel that I am 'growing in grace.' I have more power over temptation and over myself than I had some time since. But I want the witness of full sanctification. I want faith to lay hold. When I am pleading with God, I feel that I believe that he is *able* to save, that he is *willing* to save, that he is able and willing to save *now*, that he *will* save; but when I strive to believe that he will save me *just now*, my heart shrinks back. This last act of faith, I think, must be of the immediate operation of the Spirit. Lord, fill me with love!

"Friday, October 6th. Right glad was I when reading the minutes of last Conference to find that this day was appointed to be observed throughout the Connexion as a day of fasting and prayer. In two meetings that I have already attended I felt much of the presence of God. I accept this as is token that God will hear the thousands of prayers that are offered up this day, and will send us prosperity throughout the Connexion. But though I have spent above three hours on my knees this day, I still feel a reluctance to private prayer. Since last Friday, I have been excessively harassed with wandering thoughts in private prayer, and very rarely have I conquered. No sooner have I reclaimed my mind from one object than it has been after another; and even while my lips have been asking for deliverance from wandering thoughts, my mind has been elsewhere. This ceaseless combat is, perhaps, one reason that I feel such reluctance to this duty. I am sometimes ready to ask, 'How are these wanderings and how is this reluctance consistent with a regenerated heart? If my heart were really changed, would it be thus with me?' But I must hold my shield. My timidity also robs me of many a blessing. I sometimes have not courage to act in the will of God. At present there is one of our wealthy members sick; and though something tells me I should visit her, my foolish bashfulness restrains me. Lord, help me!

"Sunday, 8th. Tremendous Being! I wish not to presume upon thy mercy. If I do presume, be merciful to me, and satisfy my mind another way. But thou knowest I have doubts on my mind, whether I am in the right place and work. Lord, if I am right, this day give me liberty in my own soul and let some visible good be done! If I am wrong, if I have forfeited my commission, let no visible good be done and let me have no liberty, no freedom, no feeling! O Lord, let not this petition offend thee! I want above all things to please thee! Thou readest my heart.

"Wednesday, 11th. Glory be to God! This morning at the five o'clock meeting my soul was watered and blessed. I seemed to be on the verge of a full salvation. Last Sunday I had a blessed day in my own soul, but I have not yet heard of any good being done."

On the 30th of the same month he despatched a letter to Mr. Hanwell, from which the following is an extract: "I congratulate you on your increasing family. Your situation is becoming more and more responsible and important. Much depends on the father of a numerous family. Family religion is, I fear, too much neglected among us as a body of Christians. And I am afraid we do not recommend it to the people with that frequency and fervour which its importance requires. On reading Philip Henry's Life, one cannot but be struck with the diligence and earnestness with which that eminent man attended to family duties; and the consequence was that success attended his labours. May God give you and me every qualification for the right discharge of our duties as heads of families! During the Conference I began a children's meeting on Sunday afternoons and have hitherto maintained it. The matter rested rather heavily on my conscience. I promised the Conference that I would attend to this duty, but I never fulfilled my engagement until now. It requires much wisdom, patience, and firmness to instruct children." This extract furnishes an additional proof of Mr. Stoner's solicitude to discharge every part of his high office with vigilance and fidelity.

Nearly at the same time, he wrote separate letters to the different members of his father's family. Of these three only have been found. They sufficiently declare his pious anxiety for the spiritual welfare of those to whom they are addressed.

To his sister Ann he writes: "I hope you continue steadily to watch and pray. You can keep the grace of God in your heart only by attending regularly to these duties. If you omit them for one day only, it will bring coldness and deadness into your soul. You will feel more reluctant to pray than before; that reluctance will cause you to omit your duties a second day; and so on, till you lose all relish and taste and desire for spiritual things. Watch over your *tempers,* that they may be under the government of grace. Watch over your *thoughts,* that they may be exercised on good and profitable subjects. Watch over your *desires,* that you may wish for those things only that are pleasing to God. Watch over your *words,* that 'no corrupt communication may proceed out of your mouth.' Watch over your *actions,* that they may be all according to God's holy law. Watch against the *temptations of Satan,* that he may not lead you astray. Watch against *evil company;* thousands have been ruined by light and frothy companions. Watch against *'the lust of the flesh, the lust of the eyes, and the pride of life.'* Watch for *opportunities* of doing and getting good. Watch that you may pray, and pray that you may watch. By *prayer* you must get grace, and by *watching* you must keep what you have gained. May God bless you, and preserve you from every evil! So prays your affectionate brother."

"Though you are the last in the family," he writes to his sister Ellen, "you should not, on that account merely, be the least esteemed. Therefore, as I am writing a few lines to your brothers and sister, I must also devote a little time to you, or you may think it unkind. It is a great mercy that God has inclined you, in your early days, to begin to pray. Early piety is peculiarly valuable in the sight of God. The Scripture tells us, 'It is good for a man that he bear the yoke in his youth.' And God commands, 'Remember now thy Creator in the days of thy youth.' By giving your heart to God in the morning of life you will enjoy many blessings which others can never enjoy; and you will be saved from ten thousand evils which others bring on themselves through their disobedience to God's commands. Christ loves young disciples. 'He gathers the lambs with his arms, and carries them in his bosom.' Christ loves the sacrifice of a young heart. O! present him the flower in its bloom! Those who are noted in the Scriptures for their early piety are also remarked for the distinguished honour which God conferred upon them. Joseph, Samuel, David, Obadiah, Josiah, Daniel, Shadrach, Meshach, Abednego, and Timothy are some of those who remembered their Creator in their youth; and see how God honoured them. *Joseph* became the second man in Egypt and the saviour of Egypt and his father's house. *Samuel* became an eminent prophet and a judge over all the tribes of Israel. *David* was raised from the sheepfold to the throne and was the sweet singer of Israel. *Obadiah* is said to have 'feared the Lord *greatly;*' and perhaps the grand cause of this was that he feared the Lord from his *youth;* he was also one of the principal officers in King Ahab's court. *Josiah's* piety established the tottering throne of Judah for many years and brought many blessings upon the Jews. *Daniel* was raised to be the prime minister of a great empire, and his *three companions* were governors of provinces. *Timothy* was a useful bishop of a Christian church. And *Ellen Stoner*, if God should spare her and if she continue to serve him, will be a comfort to her friends, an honour to her name, useful to all around her, happy in her own soul; she will bring much glory to God and then sing his praises for ever and ever. Watch and pray. Diligently attend to private prayer. Cultivate a taste for reading. Read the Bible regularly through. Ask God before you read, and as you read, to teach you to understand his book. Keep out of light company. Improve your time. Love the house of God. Honour and obey your father and mother. Never dispute their commands. Never murmur at their directions. Pray for your sister Ann that God may keep her; for your brothers, Joseph, Thomas, and David; and for your father and mother, that God may bless them."

In writing to the different members of his father's household he did not forget the servant-boy, but addressed him in the following simple and affectionate manner: "James Gill, While I was writing to our folks, a thought struck me that I should write a line to thee also. Thou hast no kind father to take care of thee; but remember that God has promised many times in his Word to take care of the fatherless; and if thou be obedient, he will bless thee and save thee. Mind and be a good lad. Hate all sin. Nothing but sin can hurt thee. But remember, thou canst not keep thyself from sin: thou must pray to God for his grace to keep thee. Therefore, watch and pray continually. Honour and obey thy master and mistress, and I am sure they will be kind to thee as long as they live. Spend thy leisure time in reading some of those good books that thy mother has sent thee; and above all, read thy Bible. It is the book of God. It will teach thee in all things what thou must do. I will send thee thy books when I have read them, by the first opportunity. May God himself bless thee with all good things! So prays, dear Jim, thy friend, David Stoner."

"Wednesday, November 1st. I now enjoy a confidence in God. My language is, 'I the chief of sinners am, but Jesus died for me.' Were I sure of dying the next minute, this would be my language. I thank the Lord that in some things I get more power. I am enabled to be more diligent in preaching the word and visiting the sick and more spiritual in conversation; but yet I am awfully wanting in many things. I am much troubled with wandering thoughts. I do not pray enough. I am not in sufficient earnest for full sanctification. Lord, cleanse my heart! What is the reason I do not obtain this purity? I seek, and search, and ask, and ask; and yet I am without it. Since I last wrote in this diary I have been at York and was shorn of my strength. I am not at all fit to travel; it puts me out of my way, unhinges and dissipates my mind.

"Tuesday, 5th. Lord, 'I am oppressed; undertake for me!' In pity to my weakness, O help my soul! God has been laying me under fresh obligations by giving me another son and in some degree restoring my wife to health; but such is my ingratitude that my heart runs away from him. Lord, have mercy upon my wretched soul! O that I could pray! O that I could weep! O that I could repent! O that I could feel!

"Wednesday, 6th. Thank the Lord, I was a little encouraged last night. My desires were strengthened. I feel much better this morning. Come, Jesus, and take my heart!

"Friday, 8th. This morning I am resolved, by God's grace, to press forward. I feel much in my heart that is opposed to the will of God. Often there is a mighty struggle between the flesh and the spirit. May God help me to overcome!"

On the 27th and 29th of this month, he writes to Mr. Hanwell: "Praise the Lord, things are going on pretty well among us. Sinners are awakened and believers are 'built up on their most holy faith.' I never was among a people that I liked better, and we have a prospect of usefulness and prosperity. I thank the Lord with you that you and the family have been saved in the hour of affliction. Sanctified affliction can teach such lessons, and teach them so well as nothing else can. Whom the Lord loveth he chasteneth. We hear that Messrs. ——, ——, and —— are to be invited to Leeds next year. Well-chosen trio! All excellent in their kind. But which will have the brightest crown? And what other object is worthy of our pursuit? What is popularity, or learning, or extensive influence, or respectability, or honour, or anything, compared with bringing glory to God in promoting the salvation of sinners? I might as well ask, What is a straw, or a bubble, or a butterfly, when compared with an empire? May God help you and me to keep the right object in view and to pursue it by the best means!

"Bramwell's *Life* has done much good in this neighbourhood. What a man of prayer and faith was he! Is it possible to attain the same intimacy and power with God that he enjoyed? I believe it is, if we are willing to pay the same price for it. He lived perpetually in the spirit of sacrifice. A great deal, I find from my own experience, is implied in being willing to receive salvation on Christ's own terms. I wish to enjoy his perfect love; but I often wish to have other things at the same time that are inconsistent with it. This is one reason why I do not receive it. Pray for me, that I may in all things subdue my natural timidity. This has robbed me of thousands of blessings. Sometimes I am ready to think, had I such an easy, open, cheerful, free temper as Mr. Hanwell or some other men that I know, how much easier would it be for me to reprove sin, to introduce spiritual conversation, to visit the sick and poor, etc. But I know that to murmur is impious. I thank God, I think I become less rusty and reserved every year; and if I could but get the whole mind that was in Christ, this would be the greatest assistant to me. May the Lord wholly sanctify my soul!

"Wednesday, January 3rd, 1821. I have entered on a new year. The last year, on the whole, was certainly the best of my life. Praise the Lord, O my soul! God has blessed me in my own soul, in my family, and in my labours. All glory to him! I have entered on this year with a desire to live more to him. I feel my soul at full stretch for all his fulness.

"Tuesday, 23rd. Praise the Lord, I feel my soul alive. My heart is going out after him. This morning, while at the footstool of my Father's throne, I clearly saw that I had been living for two objects instead of living for one alone. I have been striving to please God and to please self, instead of living only for God. These two objects have occupied my attention, at different times, throughout the day. This is one reason why I have so often found the service of the Lord a cross. Whilst I have been engaged in acts of the Lord's service, I have been wishing they were over, that I might again be pleasing my other master. Lord, forgive me! Help me to live for thee alone! To this end, convince me that it is my duty and privilege to do everything for thee and to aim at thy glory every minute of every day. Bless me with divine recollectedness, that I may always remember the objects for which I ought to live; and give me grace that I may resolutely do thy will in spite of every obstruction. Lord, fully save my soul!"

In the beginning of this year, he had a dispute with the players, of which he has given the following account in a letter to Mr. Hanwell, dated February 28th: "We have had in our town a delightful hurly-burly with the players. A few Sundays since, the playhouse stumbled in my way as I was preaching in Bradford; and I honoured it with a few foul names, such as, a nest of corruption, a synagogue of Satan, a nursing mother for harlots and thieves, etc., etc. During the following week the manager called upon me to inquire why I had abused his *respectable, moral, useful,* and *authorized* profession; and to threaten me that if I dared to say another word on that subject, he would hold me up to public contempt and give me all the punishment due to my *ungentlemanly* conduct that the law would afford, etc. We had a conversation of some length. He defended the playhouse in *theatricals* and I objected in *canonicals*. He stormed and raged several times and swore that he would come to the chapel on the following

Sabbath; and if I dared to say a word against his profession, in plain Yorkshire, I should catch it. I advised him by all means to come. He went to consult an attorney to know what he could do, but met with no encouragement. He has also been to the magistrates, but can find no relief. For a few days this affair made quite a bustle in the town. Reports said that the manager was sending me a writ, that I was taken before the magistrates, that I was going to gaol, etc., etc. To blow the spark into a flame and increase the bustle, I got fifteen hundred copies of a paper printed, entitled, 'Why don't you go to the play?' and circulated them through the town. It was immediately reported that the manager was about to answer it, but he has been wise enough to be silent. On the following Sunday, Mr. Entwisle said something on the subject. Since then, the vicar, the Independent minister, and Dr. Steadman have all been talking against the theatre. We hear that the players can hardly subsist. One evening, it is certain, they did not perform, as they had only seven present. And on the manager's benefit night, they did not receive as much as paid expenses."

It seems that the threat which Mr. Stoner had received was partly executed. One of the comedians composed a piece of poetry and recited it in the playhouse. In this precious document, Mr. Stoner is styled "a fanatical cur with more vengeance than grace, an insolent cur, like the dog in the manger, a bombastical elf"; and his preaching is denominated "hypocritical canting." In these courtly expressions consist all the wit and all the poetry of this marvellous piece. The players had mistaken their man; and their feeble efforts to expose him to contempt would doubtless have excited his mirth if that had not been subdued by a feeling of pity for their grovelling principles and mental imbecility. His opposition to them appears to have been successful. They returned to the town two or three of the following winters; but, not finding themselves able to establish an interest, they at length abandoned the place. The building which they occupied is now appropriated to other uses.

"The work," he adds in the same letter, "is going on tolerably in our Circuit. There is a great revival of the spirit of hearing, and this has led to the conviction and conversion of a few scores of souls. I hope to see a mighty and a general shower. And I trust we shall have a good increase this year, both in our Circuit and throughout the connexion at large. 'Our fathers, where are they? and the prophets, do they live for ever?' Your old friend Mr. Samuel Taylor is gone home. We hear that Mr. Gates too is dead. Death breaks in upon us. May God make you and me ready! Remember me at the throne of grace. Pray for me, that I may be 'filled with all the fruits of righteousness' and rendered useful in the church!" In this letter he mentions a project which he had indulged of composing a little book containing "hints or advice to the young." A small portion of this he appears to have written, and it is a matter of regret that he never executed his intention. Such a work, from one of his judgment and piety—and one too who had been early accustomed to the tuition of youth—would undoubtedly have proved both acceptable and useful.

"Wednesday, May 2nd. 'I am oppressed: undertake for me!' What must I do? To whom can I turn but to my God? He has the words of endless life! O my Jesus, give me the power to deny self and live to thee!

"Thursday, September 20th. What is now the state of my mind! Do I now enjoy an interest in Christ? Am I a child of God? It is suggested that I have not repented enough for my past unfaithfulness. To this I answer, My acceptance with God does not depend on the *degree* of my repentance. It is suggested that I have been guilty of many imperfections, omissions of duty, sins, etc. To this I answer, This alone cannot hinder me from being a child of God. Do I now feel willing to sell all? Do I hate sin? Am I resolved, by the grace of God, to avoid it? I am. I do hate sin. I feel I hate it more than I did some time since. I feel willing, as far as I know myself, to sell all so that I may win Christ. I am conscious that I am a sinner; that I have been 'the chief of sinners;' but I hate my sins. I come to Christ. I know he loved me and gave himself for me.' He is able and willing to save. I trust in him. I depend on him. I give myself to him. I take him as my Saviour. I call him *mine*. I call myself *his*. I feel a considerable degree of delight in prayer, in reading his Word, in spiritual conversation. I can often, in some measure, keep my mind recollected; and I feel a desire for the prosperity of Zion. But O, what a wicked heart I have! Self-denial I am greatly deficient in. I can sit for hours reading and receiving fresh notions, and neglect prayer, visiting the sick, etc. I resolve, by the grace of God helping me, to lay down any book *instantly* when I feel that it is gaining an ascendancy over me. Lord, help!

"Friday, 21st. I feel that I am the Lord's. And since he is mine and I am his, what can I want beside? I only want to be unreservedly his. At prayer and in reading the Word I am guilty of wandering thoughts; and what is still worse, I do not feel enough on account of such wanderings. When I have members to cross out, I am sorry; but I fear the principal cause of my sorrow is that we have our numbers in this Circuit reduced; so, on the contrary, when we receive new members. I want my heart entirely renewing; it is deceitful above all things!

"Saturday, 22nd. Last night, in secret prayer, my heart was drawn out in fervency; but how soon do I forget all again! My heart starts aside like a broken bow. I walk, and talk, and read, and sometimes forget God. O! what an evil heart of unbelief! Create in me a clean heart!

"Monday, 24th. Yesterday, on the whole, I had a good day. In going to Low Moor in the morning, I had a strong conflict about reproving Sabbath-breakers. Some I passed by and said nothing, but at last I got courage and reproved many. Though I was laughed at and ridiculed, I felt unutterable sweetness, especially when I read these words in the lesson: 'Rejoicing that they were counted worthy to suffer shame for his name.' In the evening, being in company, I lost much spirituality by wishy-washy conversation, and grieved myself by an unguarded expression. Lord, help me! My trust is in thee! Thou art my helper! I finished reading the Rev. Henry Martyn's *Life* this morning. What a worm am I compared with that giant!

"Wednesday, 26th. The Lord still preserves my soul alive. Praise to his name! I seek this perfect love, yet cannot receive it. I feel I am growing in grace. I feel more willing to be anything or nothing. But I am far from being what I ought to be. I want the love of Christ to *constrain* me to pray without ceasing, to rejoice evermore, to live in the spirit of sacrifice, to love my brethren and all men for Christ's sake. O give me this *constraining* love! At the five o'clock meeting this morning, I expected, but received not.

"Thursday, 27th. This morning I did not feel that spirituality of mind, that intenseness of desire, which I have felt; but in prayer my strength was renewed. My evil heart of unbelief is prone to leave my God. I sometimes detect its pride and selfishness and enmity, etc. Yesterday, Satan tempted me to neglect a cross that was laid before me—visiting the sick; and for a moment I felt in a yielding position, but by the grace of God I conquered. This morning I have been reading, 'Likewise reckon ye also yourselves to be dead indeed unto sin, but alive unto God through Jesus Christ our Lord;' and I have been striving to reckon *myself* 'dead to sin' and 'alive to God.'

"Saturday, 29th. Went to Bankfort last night. A few friends accompanied me. We had some profitable conversation, but how hard it is to talk and not hurt one's self! Pride was a motive that induced me to say something, and I spoke evil of an absent person. I feel an increasing hatred to pride. I feel almost impatient to be saved from pride. I want to feel that I am worse than the worst, less than the least, and that *Christ* is *all* in *all*. I fasted yesterday and spent some time in prayer and self-examination, but yet I cannot lay hold on this perfect love.

"Monday, October 1st. I had a pretty good day at Horton yesterday. A friend told me that I set the standard of Christian perfection too high. I think not. However, I must examine my Bible. I felt envy and pride strongly stirring last night. As the watchman watches for the morning, so is my soul waiting for the fulness of love."

Of the conversation which he had with the friend above-noted on the subject of Christian perfection, he gives a more detailed account in a letter to Mr. Hanwell, of the same date: "I was yesterday preaching from Matt. 5:8: 'Blessed are the pure in heart: for they shall see God!' One of my hearers, a very sensible man, thinks that I set the standard of Christian purity too high—higher than the Bible, Messrs. Wesley and Fletcher, and experience set it. I contended, for instance, that in a justified person, on certain occasions anger may be felt rising in the heart; yet by the grace of God he keeps it down; but that in a person wholly sanctified, *every remnant of the disposition to anger* is destroyed, and that, in the greatest provocations, his mind is easy, unruffled, and calm. He may feel grieved and sorry on account of the sins of those that provoke him, but no anger; and this *grief of mind* is what is meant by holy anger: 'Be ye angry, and sin not.' 'He looked round on them with *anger*, being *grieved f*or the hardness of their hearts.' But my friend reasoned that a man in the highest state of grace must feel something rising in his mind at times, some vestige of an evil temper; otherwise he could have no temptation, and there would be no possibility of his falling. In answer to this, I appealed to the experience of Christ—He had no evil temper, and yet he was tempted; and to that of *Adam*—he was entirely holy, and yet he was tempted and fell. He then referred to a letter of Mr. Wesley's (*Works*, vol. xii., p. 271) which you may read, where he mentions *ill-judged zeal* and an *excess of affection*, etc. I still contended that those tempers mentioned by Mr. Wesley were not sinful—that they did not prove any want of perfect love, but rather arose from an excess of it—that they originated in a want of knowledge and not in a want of holiness. But, like most disputants, we ended where we began. I am still of the same mind. For this blessing of spiritual purity I am seeking; and I wish not to throw any hindrance in my own way, or in the way of others, by setting the mark too high. Give me your thoughts."

In this debate, as in most others, what seems to have been chiefly wanting was a proper explanation or adjustment of terms. Very possibly, too, Mr. Stoner, in the ardour of his zeal and the energy of his desires, might sometimes use language scarcely consistent with the frailties of our present mortal condition.

In the letter which has furnished the above extract he has some useful observations on preaching to the unconverted: "Have you seen the Rev. W. Ward's *Farewell Letters?*[1] If you have not, and can borrow them for sixpence, borrow them; or if you want a fund of missionary speeches, buy them. In those letters there is one subject which has often occupied my attention, urged, I think, *to the extreme;* namely, *preaching to the unconverted.* Mr. Ward pleads that every church ought to support *an evangelist*, whether it can support a *pastor* besides or

---

1 William Ward, *Farewell Letters to a Few Friends in Britain and America, on Returning to Bengal in 1821.*

not—that the converted will find what they need of instruction, etc., in the other means of grace if the pulpit is employed wholly in addresses to the unconverted. Now this is certainly going to an extreme. The bulk of the Christian church has indeed wandered very far into the opposite extreme, of confining public discourses to the religious professor; and therefore it is no marvel if Mr. Ward, considering his character and circumstances, has overstepped the line on the other side. This is a subject that I could love to see, or hear, ably discussed. I have had some thoughts of writing a short piece for the *Magazine* for the purpose of exciting a discussion—the purport of which piece should be to inquire how large a part of our public discourses should be addressed to the unconverted. I think at least *one half* of our texts and sermons should lead that way. There are preachers who very seldom deliver a sermon on sin, or death, or hell, or judgment, or the law, or repentance, or the threatenings, or anything that is awful and terrible. I have remarked that those preachers are generally the most useful who give the greatest prominence in their sermons to these subjects, and that as men advance in life they are apt to dwell less on such topics. Dr. Watts says, 'I never knew but one person in the whole course of my ministry who acknowledged that the first motions of religion in his own heart arose from a sense of the goodness of God. But I think all besides who have come within my notice have rather been first awakened by the passion of fear to flee from the wrath to come.' I intend, when I have an opportunity, to hear Mr. Entwisle's opinion on these subjects. Now, give me your animadversions or illustrations."

"Tuesday, 23rd. Since I wrote here last, I have had a severe attack of fever; but the Lord, in answer to the prayers of his people, has rebuked the disorder and restored me. I am afraid I have gained nothing by this affliction. I felt my mind dissipated, and I was interrupted in my usual proceedings. But I again enjoy the drawings of the Spirit. Last night, while Mr. Entwisle was preaching, my soul was greatly blessed.

"Wednesday, 31st. The Lord occasionally fetters me with bad times in preaching, or I should wax fat and kick. The two last evenings I have felt as if almost left to myself in preaching. Lord, humble me, and show me what is in my heart! I have had a pretty good time this morning at the five o'clock meeting. 'Revive thy work!'

"Sunday, November 4th. I had a blessed meeting last night. The Lord is visiting us again. My soul is alive. I feel more power with God. May he fill me and use me for his glory this day!

"Friday, 9th. My soul is still seeking for perfect liberty. O when will the day of freedom arrive? Come, Lord Jesus!

"Monday, 12th. I want two great blessings: first, my soul filling with love; and secondly, the abiding witness that I am fully sanctified. Yesterday I saw one of Bishop Beveridge's resolutions, which I should like to act upon: 'I will not speak much, lest I should speak too much; and I will not speak at all unless I can speak to purpose.' I feel I am 'growing in grace.' I have more power to deny myself, to pray constantly, and to live to God. But yet I am far, very far behind.

"Tuesday, 20th. Glory be to God! Glory be to God! This morning I have been able to draw very near the throne. I brought the *promise* and the *blood* in the hand of faith. I gave up all to God. I got hold of Christ. I remembered Mr. Fletcher's words, 'that it is better to be condemned for believing wrong than for not believing at all.' I therefore believed that Christ was wholly mine and that I was wholly his; and I felt a calm and sweetness in my inmost soul. In reading, I met with the passage, 'He cannot deny himself;' and these words came to my mind, 'According to thy faith it shall be done to thee.' Well, then, I am fully the Lord's and the Lord is fully mine. Glory be to God! Now, my Lord, give me power to live a moment at once, and that moment simply looking to Jesus!

"Friday, 23rd. Yesterday I enjoyed, on the whole, a pretty good day. I could, in some degree, keep my mind fixed. But in the evening I had an awkward affair to examine. One of our members is accused of acting improperly, and I am afraid the accusation is too true. As I had this to hear before preaching, it deadened my soul when I had to stand up. I am almost ready to say, The more I know of the professing church the less I see to approve. But let me look to my own heart and life, and I may say, with the greatest propriety, The more I know of them, the less I must approve. The devil pursues me throughout the day with horrid temptation; and I am sometimes afraid that, for a moment, I am off my guard and indulge temptations. But the Lord knows my heart. He knows that I hate sin and that I wish to be wholly his. I was up this morning at half past five and was on my knees about an hour; but notwithstanding my prayers, etc., I feel as if I could not get off the spot; nay, sometimes I think I am losing instead of gaining.

"Saturday, 24th. I had a good time at Bankfoot last night. In urging perfect love, I tasted a drop myself; and likewise at prayer before I went to the pulpit. This morning I prayed as usual, but I did not get that nearness to the throne I wish for. I feel constantly in danger of having my mind dissipated from the centre, even by sermons, good books, etc. 'Come, Lord Jesus, come quickly!'

"Wednesday, 28th. This morning I enjoy peace within. Yet I do not feel that burning, earnest, restless desire for more love and for the salvation of souls for which I long. Praise the Lord, I have more power to live to him and love him and do his will than I had. Keep me, my Lord, keep me! I met two classes last night that are decreasing. O how discouraging! Lord, undertake for us!

"Friday, 30th. I yesterday felt all my old listlessness creeping over me, so that this morning I had little heart to pray. But, by the help of the Lord, I got pretty near the throne, and I now feel my soul greatly quickened. Lord, keep me alive!

"Saturday, December 1st. I had a pretty good day yesterday. Took tea at a friend's and had a spiritual visit. I have endeavoured of late, where I could do it, to hold a sort of class-meeting after tea at these little parties and have found the advantage of it.

"Wednesday, 5th. At the five o'clock meeting this morning my soul was quickened and blessed. And I had great need of it. On Sunday I had a good day, but was sorely harassed with temptation in the evening, *before* preaching, with doubts and fears that I should not get through; and *afterwards* with the thought, what a good sermon I had preached. O, I want this perfect love. Then I should feel more love to prayer, to the Word, and to the work of the Lord. Sometimes I feel a backwardness to prayer. I feel a call to pray, and then something suggests, 'Wait till thou hast done such a thing.' But I feel determined always to stop, if I can, and *there* and *then* to pray.

"Thursday, 6th. O the necessity of being faithful with the sick! I was called this day to see a poor dying man. He could hardly speak, and seemed as ignorant of salvation as a post. I talked and prayed with him and he died in the course of an hour. 'Deliver me from blood-guiltiness, O God, thou God of my salvation!'"

At this time his excellent mother was labouring under the ravages of a cancer in the breast, which in the end terminated her valuable life. She was now from home for the benefit of medical advice. To her he writes on the fifth of this month in the following pious and affectionate terms: "How comfortable is the thought that we are in the hands of our Father! 'Like as a father pitieth his children, so the Lord pitieth them that fear him.' He is too wise to do wrong and too good to be unkind. All his designs concerning them that love him are gracious and merciful, and we would act just as he does if we had as much knowledge as he has. 'Blessed are all they that trust in him.'

"You beg an interest in our prayers. Be assured that if my poor prayers can do anything, you shall have them. You were never for a day forgotten whilst you were in health; and much more do I feel for you and pray for you now that the Lord has put you into the furnace. But remember, you are not put into the fire to be consumed and destroyed, but to be tried and purified and made white. 'Tribulation worketh patience; and patience, experience; and experience, hope.' And these 'light afflictions, which are but for a moment, are working out for you a far more exceeding and eternal weight of glory.'

"You must strive, mother, to leave all Barwick concerns at Barwick, and Bradford affairs at Bradford, and Dudley Hill[1] anxieties at Dudley Hill for the present. If you are ever so anxious about the family, I do not think it will add one mite of efficacy to the medicines, etc. The best way is to carry all our concerns and care to him who takes charge of the sparrows and hears the young ravens when they cry. The hairs of our heads are all numbered; and if God takes notice of our very hairs, we are sure that so important a thing as a cancer cannot escape his knowledge. Yea, it is sent by him, and sent in mercy too. He says, 'What thou knowest not now, thou shalt know hereafter.' Then,

---

1   Where a brother of Mr. Stoner's had recently opened a school.

> Judge not the Lord by feeble sense,
> But trust him for his grace!
> Behind a frowning providence,
> He hides a smiling face.

May the eternal God be your refuge, and underneath be his everlasting arms! May he 'fill you with all joy and peace in believing;' and after all the storms of life are over, may he conduct us safely to that land the inhabitant of which shall never say, 'I am sick;' and where 'God shall wipe away all tears from our eyes!' Amen, and Amen. So prays your affectionate and sympathizing son."

"Saturday, 8th. Lord, help me now to examine my heart and describe the state of my mind. Yesterday, in reading the life of that excellent man, Dr. Doddridge, my soul was humbled, softened, and quickened. I resolved, by God's grace, to begin again. I feel greater delight in spiritual conversation and more power to deny myself of light reading and unnecessary sleep, to visit the sick and poor, to cultivate spirituality of mind, and to maintain the spirit of prayer, than I formerly did. For this I praise thee, O God! But still, I do not eat and drink for God's glory. I do not 'set the Lord always before me.' Sometimes there are long intervals in which I am not engaged with God. I do not 'pray without ceasing.' I do not 'for everything give thanks.' I do not watch against idle thoughts sufficiently. My secret devotions are often marred with wanderings. I do not feel that relish for prayer and for the Word which I ought to do. I am not so useful in my public labours, on three accounts, as I ought to be: 1. I do not follow up public preaching by pastoral visits and personal conversation. 2. I do not pray before and after preaching for success as I ought to do. 3. I do not, as I ought, simply and solely rely on the Holy Spirit, without whom all sermons are vain. I often feel the risings of pride and many roots of bitterness. But what must I do? Whither can I go but to thee, my Saviour! 'Open thy arms, and take me in!' I resolve, by divine grace: 1. To spend less time in sleep. 2. To spend more time on my knees. 3. To guard more against wandering thoughts, especially in my devotions. 4. To avoid idle conversation. 5. To attend more to pastoral visits. 6. To be more thankful. 7. To take some text every morning for the occupation of my mind at intervals.

Lord, help me! Thou knowest my feebleness. These resolutions, like thousands before, will be broken if thou dost not help me. Now, take my heart! In my devotions this morning I have felt enlargement and nearness in my intercessions and in reading the Word.

"Monday, 10th. I had yesterday a pretty good day. In my morning devotions I felt a little enlargement of heart. In going to Bingley I was enabled to keep my mind pretty well fixed on spiritual subjects. I was assaulted with some horrid temptations, but cried to God. Tolerable liberty in the morning; felt assaulted with pride afterwards. Heard evil-speaking and did not reprove it as I should have done. Humbled myself before God for my cowardice. Good time in the evening; tempted of pride. In returning, I had not my mind properly engaged. This morning have had my mind again dissipated through different engagements, but felt nearness to the throne in prayer, and wish to live to God. Lord, help me this day!

"Tuesday, 11th. I felt yesterday anger and peevishness still existing in my heart. I strove and prayed against them. Yet I did not 'pray without ceasing.' I wasted many intervals in wandering imaginations. This morning I have felt a considerable degree of nearness to the throne.

"Wednesday, 12th. At the prayer-meeting this morning, I felt in earnest. 'I dare believe in Jesu's name' was the language of my heart. O for the fulness of love! Saw a young man yesterday very ill in body but worse in mind. 'It is too late,' said he. 'I have no hope. I cannot believe the Bible. I have disbelieved the Bible. I have read the Bible again and again, and done it only with the intention of finding faults in it,' etc. I endeavoured to reason with him, but everything I could say he turned against himself. I urged him to make a trial of Jesus Christ, whether his word was true or not. He has been accounted a steady, moral young man, has attended the church, and was not known to be a disbeliever. But now he thinks himself to be the worst sinner that ever lived.

"Thursday, 13th. Much unwatchfulness had brought deadness into my soul, but in prayer this morning the fire was kindled again. Lord, help me to watch this day!

"Sunday, 16th. Yesterday I was assaulted with powerful temptation; but getting last night into an agony of prayer, I, in a great measure, found deliverance. This morning I got very near the throne. I gave up all. I felt a fresh application of the blood of Christ. I felt as if I was within a hair's breadth of God's whole salvation, but I cannot say I received it. Still I feel my mind in perfect peace. O my God and my all! be with me through this day!

"Wednesday, 19th. This morning I went to the meeting expecting to meet with Jesus. I felt fully in earnest. I felt the spirit of agonizing prayer, but yet I could not lay hold. Lord, have mercy on my soul! Surely I shall not carry my old heart into the new year. Praise the Lord, I feel more power to deny self. I got hold of a bewitching book yesterday; but I felt that the tendency of it would be to draw me away from God, and he enabled me to deny self.

"Friday, 21st. The devil follows me hard with horrid temptations, and I often fear that I do not resist them with sufficient abhorrence. When I feel them, I wish to start with alarm as much as if I saw the house on fire. To have to preach to sleepy folks and half-hearted folks has a very damping, deadening effect on my mind. O that I could constantly live on full stretch after God! I want a more spiritual mind. On examining myself this morning, I do not know that I have anything contrary to love in my heart; but I want to be filled with God. I was much encouraged yesterday while pleading the words of St. John, 'This is the confidence that we have in him, That if we ask anything according to his will, he heareth us; and if we know that he hear us, whatsoever we ask, we know that we have the petitions that we desired of him.' To ask according to his will seems to us to mean to ask for all things that are pleasing to him and to ask in an acceptable manner. Now, I have asked for a clean heart; and I am as sure that this is according to his will as that I am alive; and I labour to ask in a manner pleasing to him—in humility, in earnestness, in the name of Christ, in faith. And if I can thus ask, I know that I have the petitions that I desired of him. O for the power of faith!"

To Mr. Hanwell, under the date of December 22nd, he writes: "You say, 'I find it profitable to read a portion of some pious work before private prayer.' I have often done something of the same kind.

There is nothing I can read which produces so much effect on my mind as religious biography; and I have found it beneficial to have some work of this kind lying by me, that I may occasionally mingle a page or two of it among my other employments through the day, in order to stimulate myself to greater earnestness and diligence and to render my mind more spiritual. I have of late more than ever seen the evil of idle discourse; and yet, alas, too often have I been betrayed into it. But I ought to say too, to the glory of divine grace, that I have been enabled more fully to keep a watch over my tongue than formerly; and I have felt the benefit of it. I have been at several tea parties lately among our rather lower class of friends, where I have been the chairman, so to speak. After tea, I have held a sort of class-meeting, and then got all the friends present to pray; and I have thus enjoyed some profitable seasons.

"I sometimes find it difficult to maintain a regular course of self-denial. The flesh and the devil struggle hard; but I hope to conquer. Help me by your fervent prayers. When I review my past life, I am ashamed and humbled; and I grieve that I cannot review it with more abhorrence, detestation, and self-loathing. I cannot find words strong enough to express what I ought to feel on the recollection of my ingratitude, disobedience, and thousand sins. And yet—would you believe it?—I often have temptations to pride; yea, such a temptation have I had while I have been writing the last two or three lines—to be *proud* of my *expressions of humility*. But with these views of myself I do not feel that self-annihilation and that thankfulness for the infinite mercy of my God which I wish to do. I am a riddle to myself. I possess a confidence in Christ as my Saviour; yet O how little I love him! I have a strong desire to enjoy the fulness of the gospel; yet when I come to pray, O how often am I pestered with wandering thoughts! 'I hate myself, and yet I love.' I love my Saviour, and yet I often slight him. I pray for the Spirit, and yet I often grieve the Spirit. 'O that I had wings like a dove! for then would I fly away, and be at rest.'"

"Saturday, December 22nd. Praise the Lord! I have been examining myself this morning, and I do not feel anything, that I know of, contrary to love. While at prayer, these words in the morning lesson seemed to suit my case: 'Sing and rejoice, O daughter of Zion: for lo, I come, and I will dwell in the midst of thee, saith the Lord. Behold, I have caused thine iniquity to pass from thee, and I will clothe thee with change of raiment.' Surely it shall be done! Come, Lord, and come quickly!

"Wednesday, 26th. Yesterday morning at the five o'clock meeting I had a precious visit from the Lord. In the forenoon, while preaching at Clayton, I had a very good time. In the afternoon, at the missionary meeting, my heart was melted within me. But at tea time my soul was wounded with light conversation. Lord, have mercy on me!

"Thursday, 27th. In examining myself this morning I discovered many awful deficiencies. 1. The Lord found me in bed when I ought to have been on my knees and at my work. 2. I did not devote my first thoughts to him. 3. I have suffered roving imaginations to engage my mind while reading the Word and on my knees. 4. I have been formal in my family duties. 5. I have not prayed with my wife as I intend to do. 6. I do not mourn over sin as I ought to do. 7. I do not 'pray without ceasing.' 8. I do not 'in everything give thanks.' 9. I do not live in the recollection of God's presence. 10. Unbelief, worldly-mindedness, envy, and self-will are things that have often conquered me. 11. I have spoken many idle words. 12. I do not eat and drink for the glory of God. 13. I do not pray every hour for a revival. I was grieved that I did not feel more grief. I endeavoured to confess my sins and humble myself, and again I laid hold on Christ. I resolve, by God's help, to do better. Mrs. Fletcher's words suited me. Once she hesitated to say that she was the 'chief of sinners.' I have often felt the same hesitation. But I thank my Lord, I am getting lower thoughts of myself. Sink down, my soul! Break my stony heart! Flow, my eyes, with penitential tears!

"Wednesday, January 2nd, 1822. What a mercy that I see a new year! The last has been marked, every moment of it, with loving-kindness. I closed the year at Horton Chapel, and a precious meeting we had. I gave myself to God. In private prayer this morning I have got a little nearer the throne. I see there is a full salvation through Christ for me. Christ is mine, and therefore this salvation is mine. I claim it, and I urge my claim. If I had an estate that was possessed by some usurper, I should still call it mine; and I should urge my claims till I was put in possession. So here I hold. I have not the full possession, but it is mine. O for faith! O for power!

"Friday, 4th. This is the day of the quarterly fast. Lord, pour upon me the spirit of prayer, of deep humiliation, and of faith. I intend to devote the greater part of this day to meditation, self-examination, reading the Word, prayer, and praise. Let me begin with self-examination and a confession of my sins to God."

He then enters into a minute and severe investigation of his tempers, words, and actions during his past life, after which he proceeds thus: "And of all this wickedness have I been guilty, notwithstanding the advantages I have enjoyed. In my earliest days, my parents instructed me, chastised me, restrained me, brought me up in attendance on the means of grace. God called me in early life to seek him. I had 'line upon line, precept upon precept.' In my situations, I had every spiritual advantage; and yet I have been thus wicked. I have sinned against the mercy of the Father, the blood of the Son, the strivings of the Spirit, the remonstrances of my own conscience, the convictions of my own mind. I have sinned against thee, O my God, against my own body and soul, against my fellow-creatures, against the law, and against the gospel, against light and knowledge. I have sinned in action, in thought, in word, in motive, in desire. My sins are more numerous than the hairs on my head, numberless as the sands on the seashore, infinitely aggravated! What must I do? O my heart, break into pieces! Ye tears of contrition, flow! I would mourn before the Lord. I would mourn that I mourn so little. I would repent of my repentance. O my Lord! whatever thou givest or withholdest beside, give me a broken and a contrite heart! Give me true repentance, and help me to loathe myself on account of my sins! Help me to 'repent as in dust and ashes!' I am the worst of sinners. I am the very chief of rebels. Lord, humble my soul. All these sins I have committed, notwithstanding the obligations under which I have been laid, the favours with which I have been blessed, the vows that I have made, the covenants into which I have entered, the manifestations of love that I have had, and the answers to prayer that I have often received! Lord, be merciful to me a sinner! Whither can I go? To the Saviour!

Christ has died—He has died for me! He assumed our nature, was born in a stable, and laid in a manger; and he rested his infant head on hay, his dying head on thorns; his cradle was the manger and the cross his deathbed. Three-and-thirty years of suffering and pain did he endure for me—for my sins! I come to the door of mercy. Here I'll knock, I'll wait, I'll beg. If I stay away, I am undone. If I come, at the worst I am but undone! But I shall not be cast out. God has commanded me to come. Lord, I come. If thou wert to send me to hell, it would be all just. But in the hand of faith, I bring the blood, the blood! I am a sinner, but here is the blood! Justice says, 'Cut him down;' but here is the blood! Satan says, 'He belongs to me;' but here is the blood! This blood is mine; this Saviour is mine. I look to him. I see him weeping, bleeding, dying for me. Here is love! Here is love!

> Love so amazing, so divine,
> Demands my life, my soul, my all!

Lord, take all! my body, soul, time, family, property, my all! Do with me what thou wilt; put me where thou wilt; use me as thou wilt; only let thy name be glorified, and let my soul be filled with love. I am thine and thou art mine. What can I want beside? Glory be to God! I roll all my sins on Jesus, and take him as my 'wisdom, righteousness, sanctification, and redemption.' Glory be to God! I praise him for my parents, senses, food, raiment, habitation, family mercies, bodily and spiritual mercies; for the deliverances he has wrought out, the promises he has made, the answers to prayer, the blessings he has bestowed, the grace he has given; for the mercies of the past year, and the comforts of this new year. Glory be to God! But still I want more grace. I want a clean heart, a right spirit, a stayed mind. I want his perfect love. All I want is included in love, perfect love. And he says, 'Only believe; all things are possible to him that believeth.' Glory be to God, I do believe. I believe this salvation is provided for me, held out to me. I lay claim to it as mine! It is mine, for Christ is mine. I urge my claim. I want to feel the possession of it. I want to feel all peace, all calm, all love. Come, Lord Jesus, come quickly! Praise the Lord, I have had two good prayer-meetings. The presence of the Lord was among us, softening and melting my heart. I hope we shall see still better days. Two such prayer-meetings we had before the last revival. During the past quarter we have lost many wanderers. O may the Lord in mercy reclaim them! Praise the Lord! Nearly seven hours in succession I have spent on my knees, and have felt it good to draw near to God. Lord, help me to live praying, watching, believing, loving, obeying, or I shall receive no benefit.

"Saturday, 5th. I had indeed a good day yesterday; and this morning, while on my knees, I had a precious visit from above. I had been considering the words of Christ, 'What things soever ye desire, when ye pray, believe that ye receive them, and ye shall have them.' Now I ask for a clean heart. I know it is according to the will of God, and I ask in the name of Christ.

"Monday, 7th. Yesterday, upon the whole, I had a good day. I had an opportunity of renewing my covenant with God, and I think I freely gave up all. This morning I have had particular power to plead and to believe for a clean heart. The blessing is mine. I now believe. But O, I want the fulness! Lord, help me to live to thee!

"Wednesday, 9th. Last night we had a good watch-night at Clayton heights, and this morning a good meeting. But how is it that we do not receive the mighty baptism for which we pray? Lord, help us to believe. I feel faith in my God. I am determined 'obstinately' to believe, as Mr. Fletcher has it. Christ is mine, and I believe I have a clean heart; but I want a clearer witness of it. O for a launch out into the deep!

"Friday, 11th. Last night I was wounded. I was suddenly attacked with very bitter language by a member of our society, and for a minute I did not recollect myself. I felt pride stir, and spake unadvisedly with my lips. O what a constant need of watching unto prayer!

"Saturday, 12th. Yesterday I went to ask pardon of the person to whom I had spoken rashly, and to tell him I had not spoken advisedly. Lord, help me!

"Sunday, 13th. Praise the Lord, I feel I am his. I have given myself fully to him, and taken him as my whole Saviour. While reading and praying yesterday, I felt greater power to lay hold. This sentence was applied: 'It shall be done to you according to your faith.' A ray of light seemed to shine on the way of faith, and I cried out, 'Lord, I believe.' I feel that my soul lays hold on the full salvation of God; and I believe, yea, I will believe, that it is mine. And this promise follows me: 'The Lord whom ye seek shall suddenly come to his temple.' This sentence of Mr. Fletcher penetrated my mind: 'Sink or swim, the believer must learn to plunge himself into the ocean of infinite truth and love.' Glory be to God! I do love him; I will love him. Lord, help me every moment. Last night we had a good meeting. One woman was set at liberty, two others received comfort, and a fourth struggled but did not obtain. Lord, ride on!

"Saturday, 19th. Yesterday morning I was enabled to get near the throne and to plead for the fulness of love. I laboured to believe in Christ, and I did believe. My language was, 'Lord, I *believe* this full salvation is mine, but I want to *feel* it.' Through the day, in a degree, I was in a praying frame. In the evening, after tea at Mrs. Pulman's, a few of us engaged in prayer. While Mrs. Pulman was praying, the power of the Lord came down and sweetly rested on my soul. I gave up all; I received all. I felt unutterable sweetness and joy to fill my soul. The Lord took full possession of my heart. Glory be to God! Glory be to God! I now feel a sweet calm and a breathing after the Lord. Satan tells me it is not sanctification. He says I must not call it sanctification. I answer, Whatever it is, it is love and peace and heaven and joy. Lord, help me to *walk* in the light!

"Tuesday, 22nd. I scarcely know what state I am in at present. My opinion is that I have a low degree of perfect love, viz., a clean heart. I do not know that I have felt any wrong temper rising in my heart since last Friday evening. I have felt many temptations; and sometimes it is difficult to say what springs from nature and what from Satan. I have felt many shortcomings. I cannot say that I have 'prayed without ceasing, rejoiced evermore, and in everything given thanks.' I have not habitually, every moment, had reference to the immediate presence of God. I am also conscious of many useless thoughts and words. I have, therefore, constantly to say,

> Every moment, Lord, I need
> The merit of thy death.

"I long to feel more fully given up to God. I certainly have greater power to pray and praise and believe habitually; but I want to feel that I am filled with that constraining love of Christ which will lead me every moment to devote all to God. I have much neglected the duties of visiting the sick and poor, etc. I resolve for the present to devote two hours on each of four days in the week, that is, eight hours in the week, to visiting the flock, the sick, the poor, etc., exclusively of visiting so called. I praise the Lord for some of our tea-parties lately. We have enjoyed the presence of the Lord. But O what a dwarf am I!

> Yet when melted in the flame
> Of love, this shall be all my plea,
> I the chief of sinners am,
> But Jesus died for me!

Lord, suffer me not to deceive myself! Let me not suppose that I have a clean heart and that I am thine if it is not so. I would be the Lord's. If I have a desire, it is to be filled with the love of God."

February 7th, he writes to his mother: "Dear mother, trust in the Lord and simply look to Jesus for help and comfort. Obstinately believe that he is your Saviour and that he will cause 'all things' to 'work together for your good.' Do not suppose that we forget you in our prayers. And besides our feeble petitions, millions of prayers ascend up every week for the afflicted. The people of the Lord seldom meet together without praying for the sick; and more than all, Jesus Christ prays for you; and his intercessions will prevail. May the eternal God be your refuge, your support, and your deliverer! After he has tried you awhile, may he bring you back to your family in health, to be more useful, holy, and happy, for a long series of years; until at last, like a shock of corn ripe for the garner, you are gathered home in peace!"

In a letter to Mr. Hanwell dated the 26th of the same month, he mentions one of those incidents which illustrate the peculiar power and energy of his ministry at this period. "Sunday before last I was preaching at a place in our Circuit called Clayton heights and felt considerable liberty and enlargement. As I was urging the service of the Lord upon my hearers and inquiring who would enter into it, a man in the congregation cried out that he would. His word pierced like a sword to the hearts of many so that some hundreds, I suppose, burst immediately into tears. I scarcely ever saw a congregation so affected, and I hear that many began to meet in class during the past week. If the Lord work, who shall hinder? May he ride on till all are subdued!"

At the conclusion of this letter he says, "On Tuesday evening I was preaching to a small congregation in which was an old man who suddenly died next morning. If I had foreseen this, should I not have been more earnest in preaching to him? And ought not this reflection always to accompany us, 'Perhaps I am preaching my last sermon, or some one here is listening to his last warning?'"

"During the three years," he afterwards remarks in his diary, "which I spent at Bradford, I received blessings innumerable. Eternity will be too short to tell their value. I had three years of peace and prosperity. I had the happiness of labouring with two of the excellent of the earth, Messrs. Turton and Entwisle. God gave me the hearts of the people in a remarkable degree. It is not to be described how they bore with me and loved me, nor the affection I felt for them. I never thought my contracted, selfish, stubborn disposition capable of such feelings as I have had towards the Bradford societies. To leave them was like rending my heart asunder."

He gratefully records the increase of numbers and offers a fervent prayer that "the Lord would keep them *every one!*" The attachment of the Bradford societies and congregations to Mr. Stoner was very remarkable. For a long time after his departure, his name could not be publicly mentioned without producing a powerful and visible emotion. In some instances, there can be little doubt that this attachment was carried to an undue degree and expressed in an unguarded manner. So difficult is it, in the exercise of even the best affections towards each other, to avoid inconsistencies and extremes.

The general habits of Mr. Stoner during his residence at Bradford may be discovered from the lengthened extracts which occupy many of the preceding pages. They were eminently of a self-denying kind. It was his practice to fast, in whole or in part, every Friday, and to spend not more than between six and seven hours in sleep out of the twenty-four. Perhaps in these respects he went to an extreme. His delicate constitution, and the wasting labours in which he unsparingly engaged, seem to have required more refreshment and repose than he would suffer himself to indulge. By the goodness of God, however, his health, with a few exceptions, was good; and he felt it to be his "meat and drink," his recreation and rest, to "do the will of his heavenly Father."

His fervent desire for higher attainments in the Christian life and his attention to pulpit and pastoral duties did not render him unobservant of the minuter obligations connected with his office. He was remarkably punctual and correct in everything. "In attending to his work in all its branches," says Mr. Turton, "he was one of the most exact men I ever knew—never forgetting anything I requested him to do, though mentioned to him for days, or even weeks, previous to the time of doing it." During a part of the time he spent at Bradford he filled the office of Local Secretary to the Wesleyan Academy at Woodhouse Grove, the duties of which he discharged with his wonted exactness and fidelity. At this time he also began to insert in a book, kept for the purpose, a brief record of his daily transactions—a practice which he continued until within a very short time of his death.

One thing ought not to pass, in a review of his labours at Bradford, without special notice: his deep and growing conviction of the necessity of divine influence to produce any degree of ministerial success. He attributed nothing to himself and comparatively little to the external means which he adopted. The thought that *he* was the only man to promote the interests of religion, and that the peculiar measures which *he* used were the only suitable ones, seems never to have entered his mind. He was fully satisfied that the wintry cold of spiritual indifference cannot be removed by the fires of mere human excitement; and that it is only when, in answer to humble prayer, the vernal breath of heavenly inspiration is diffused, that the frost of human nature is softened and thawed—the copious flow of new life poured forth—and the wild, desolate before and dreary, clad with new beauties, blooming "as the rose" and flourishing "like the garden of the Lord."

7

Ministry at Birstal

He contemplates a removal to Newcastle-upon-Tyne, but, for special reasons, is appointed to the Birstal Circuit—His unabated zeal and fidelity in that station—He enters upon it with a solemn dedication of himself to God—Extracts from his diary and correspondence—The death of his mother—His diary closes with a satisfactory testimony of his establishment in the divine life—The fervency of his prayers, whilst at Birstal, for the prosperity of religion—Rules for prayer-meetings—Notice of the domestic afflictions with which he now began to be visited.

Eight years had now elapsed since Mr. Stoner received his appointment at Holmfirth. During this period, his successive stations had been confined to one small section of the West Riding of Yorkshire, abounding in population and remarkable for the influence of Methodism, but not extending over a larger tract of country than is occupied by many single Circuits in other parts of the Wesleyan Connexion. To his most judicious friends it appeared desirable that he should remove to a greater distance. If there were no danger of his contracting limited views and local prejudices from a lengthened residence in the same neighbourhood, it was deemed proper that one so admirably qualified for ministerial usefulness should move in other circles and bestow the benefit of his valuable labours on other people.

Strongly as he was attached to the well-known scenes of his early exertions and success, he advanced no objection to such a removal; and on receiving an invitation from Newcastle-upon-Tyne, he consented, in submission to the openings of providence and the decision of the approaching Conference, to toil for a season in that part of the common field. So far as human judgment can pronounce, his talents would have been gratefully appreciated in that old and important Methodist station; and his zealous endeavours, aided by the blessing of God, have issued in a large portion of their wonted success. But the wishes of the Newcastle societies were not gratified. The Conference of 1822, humanely considering the declining state of his mother's health, and attending to the peculiar circumstances and wants of the Birstal Circuit, appointed him to that contiguous and retired spot. Here, in conjunction, first with the Rev. John Mercer, and afterwards with the venerable John Nelson, who has also closed his honoured career of zeal and usefulness, he spent two years of peace and prosperity.

In this situation his public duties were not of quite so trying a description as they had been in his two preceding Circuits. The chapels were comparatively small and the work easy. In some this might have produced a relaxation of effort, for human nature loves the indulgences of ease. But Mr. Stoner was governed by high and inflexible principle. Here, therefore, he laboured in prayer, in private study, and in the execution of his ministerial offices with unabated ardour and diligence. The effect of his fidelity was visible in his public ministrations. Often was the careless sinner arrested and alarmed—the penitent consoled—the Christian quickened and edified—and the callous disbeliever agitated by new emotions which he perhaps disdained to acknowledge but was compelled to feel.

No sooner was Mr. Stoner settled at Birstal than he renewed the dedication of himself to God in the following words: "Saturday, September 7th. Here, my Lord, on my knees, I enter into a solemn covenant with thee, giving my whole self to thee; promising, through thy grace, to be entirely thine; submitting to thy disposal; and claiming thee as my Father and God. As witness my hand, subscribed in thy fear and presence. DAVID STONER." Such acts of full surrender he often performed, and doubtless found them of peculiar advantage, to remind him of his obligations, to strengthen his holy purposes, and to quicken his zeal. "Glory be to God," he adds under the same date: "He is my God, therefore will I trust in him. This day I wish to consecrate to the Lord in fasting and prayer. I feel him near, producing a solemn tranquillity—a settled peace of mind."

He proceeds, "Saturday, 14th. This week has brought with it many mercies which call for thankfulness. Last Sunday was, on the whole, a good day, and I have had many profitable seasons since. But my heart is like 'a broken bow and a foot out of joint.' I want to improve every moment, to speak every word for the Lord, to have every thought regulated by his grace, to do everything to his glory. Come, Lord, and cure me now! Thou sayest, 'Give me thy heart.' It is my first desire to do it. 'If thou wilt, thou canst make me clean.' O! let it be now! This week I have been praying for three blessings: 1. The entire sanctification of my nature. 2. The revival of religion. 3. The removal of a bodily affliction under which I am labouring. The promise is, 'He will fulfil the desire of them that fear him.' Lord, 'increase my faith.' I have been striving this day to fast and pray, but my heart is cold and backward. O for the fire of holy love!

"Saturday, 21st. I now feel that I am the Lord's. I believe in Christ. This week my experience has been various. Last Saturday night I had a good meeting—the best I have had since I came into this Circuit. On Sunday I did not enjoy much liberty, nor have I had much satisfaction in preaching during the week. I have not heard, since I came, of any fruit. In approaching the 'throne of grace' today I felt cold and backward; but by perseverance in fighting against my indifference, I obtained a blessing. I long for a full salvation. Sometimes I agonize in prayer for it, but I do not live in the same spirit. In prayer, that promise recurred to my mind, 'The Lord, whom ye seek, shall suddenly come to his temple.' Lord, accomplish thy word. I throw open the doors of my heart. Take all I have. I want that *spirit* of preaching—love *to souls*. Without it, all is cold and dead. Lord, give me love to souls! It was this which constrained Jeremiah to cry out, 'O! that my head were waters, and mine eyes a fountain of tears, that I might weep day and night for the slain of the slaughter of my people!' This prompted David to say, 'Rivers of waters run down mine eyes, because they keep not thy law.' This discovered itself in that pathetic exclamation of Christ, 'O Jerusalem, Jerusalem, thou that killest the prophets, and stonest them which are sent unto thee, how often would I have gathered thy children together, even as a hen gathereth her chickens under her wings, and ye would not!' Many things in this Circuit are discouraging; but I trust that the people are engaging in prayer, and that we shall see the glory of the Lord.

"Saturday, 28th. Last Sunday, the love-feast at Gildersome was a very blessed season. A friend from Sheffield spoke and prayed, and the Lord was with us indeed and of a truth. The former part of this week was a time of prayer. Today I feel cold and languid. I have come again and again to the throne of grace, and yet I do not enjoy any liberty. I have not heard of any fruit. This will never do. I cannot be satisfied, I will not be satisfied, without fruit. Lord, help me to preach with the power of the Spirit!"

To Mr. Jennings, of whose conversion he had been the instrument, he writes, November 27th of this year, "T. A. has been again reminding me that you wish me to write to you. I thought the bargain had been that *you* were to write *first* and I afterwards. However, I will try to make a beginning. But what shall I say? I can only make general observations because I do not know the *particular* present state of your mind. I was sorry that I was so engaged the day you were over at Birstal that I could have no conversation with you; but as I am now breaking the ice for you, if, on the receipt of this, you will sit down and write to me all *how* and *about* it, I shall then be able to say something perhaps more to the purpose. I suspect that your mind is exercised on the subject of preaching. You feel a sort of hankering after it and inclination to it, and yet you start at the difficulties in the way. When you measure your own supposed unfitness for the work, you wonder at yourself for thinking about it; and, notwithstanding your wonder, you think about it still. I suspect your state to be very similar to what mine was before I began to preach. I felt moved to preach, and yet I was pretty sure I should not be able to preach extempore. I therefore thought of getting, if possible, into the established church, where I should be allowed the privilege of reading my sermons. Nothing satisfied me but a fair trial. You have heard me say I tried *twice*, and laid it aside for four months. But during that time I had no rest. I was told *twice* was not a fair trial. I began again, and in my *fifth* attempt enjoyed liberty and took courage. In my *sixth* attempt, I was more wretched in the pulpit than I have ever been, either before or since. In my *seventh*, I again enjoyed a little liberty. Now these things I mention, to convince you that mere *reasoning* on the subject in your present state of mind will

Ministry at Birstal

never produce any satisfaction. Begin, and try to preach twelve times. You will then be able to form a better judgment. But in the midst of all, live near to God. Cry to him for light and direction. Be instant and constant in prayer. Study, books, eloquence, fine sermons are all nothing without prayer. Prayer brings the *spirit*, the *life*, the *power*. Assiduously cultivate your mind. Read your Bible regularly and with prayer. Read Wesley and Fletcher. I know of no human writings like theirs. Now write to me. Tell me all your mind. Tell me what you have read—what books you have—what you are doing—how near you are living to God. Guard against temptation. Attend to St. Paul's advice to his beloved Timothy, 2 Epist. 2:22: 'Flee,' etc; not *fight*, but *flee*. A word to the wise is sufficient."

"And now, William," he observes in a letter to Mr. Gilpin, dated December 23rd of the same year, "let me remind you that *light* without *heat, knowledge* in the head without *love* in the heart, is a very unsatisfactory thing. Labour to 'grow in grace' as well as 'in knowledge.' 'The kingdom of God,' true religion, 'is not in word' only, 'but in power.' To *get* the power, there must be *strong* wrestling at the 'throne of grace;' and to *keep* it, there must be *continued* wrestling. To this all our pride, our indolence, our animal appetites and desires, our natural disrelish for spiritual things, the objects connected with the world around us, and the influence of our invisible enemies are determinately opposed. To conquer all this opposition, there must be self-denial, a violence done to our own pride, the firmest resolutions, and a dependence on divine power. May God help you to struggle and conquer!"

"Monday, March 3rd, 1824," he proceeds in his diary, "Yesterday, I had a good day. I preached three times at Birstal, administered the sacrament, and met five classes. It is not often that I have three good seasons in the pulpit in one day; however, in answer to prayer, I was at liberty all the three times. But the congregations seemed far more indifferent than I wished them to be. In the classes, I found a few who are beginning to meet. All glory to God!

"Friday, 7th. On Wednesday and Thursday evenings I conducted two missionary prayer-meetings—both well attended. This is a good sign. When the whole church shall pray earnestly, constantly, and in faith, and when they shall labour as well as pray, then will Christ save the world. My mind is drawn out after the Lord. I feel eager for the salvation of souls; but I fear that my eagerness is zeal for a party, or desire of self-exaltation, rather than true love to souls. Lord, search me!

"Saturday, 8th. This morning in prayer I have seen a great beauty in being all love. This is what I want—to be all love in my tempers, thoughts, words, designs, conversation, and conduct. In prayer, I have enjoyed liberty. Praise the Lord! I have been enabled to lay hold on Christ as my Saviour. Last night at White Lee I did not enjoy much liberty; but I heard of two who were awakened under my ministry, some time since, in that neighbourhood. To God be all the glory!

"Sunday, 9th. Last night I heard of a great sinner's being awakened when I was preaching at Bradford on Christmas Day. I feel thankful that the Lord does not cast me off, but still employs me for his glory. My Lord, go with me this day!

"Monday, 10th. Yesterday I had but little liberty in preaching. Perhaps this arose from my not having made proper preparation. I was perplexed in the choice of subjects. However, I had the pleasure of admitting twenty-seven on trial. I feel my soul going out after God. Lord, cleanse me from sin!

"Tuesday, 11th. Yesterday afternoon, in meeting a class at Morley, I was remarkably blessed. My heart was softened. The people seemed to be affected on every side. Though I do not often shed tears, I sometimes could scarcely speak for weeping. But notwithstanding this, I had a very poor time at Churwell in the evening. I am so prone to pride and self-exaltation that the Lord finds it necessary to use these means in order to keep me in my own place. Lord, have mercy upon me and cleanse my heart!

"Wednesday, 12th. I had a poor time again last night at Healey. I do not know how it is—this week I can obtain no liberty in preaching.

"Sunday, 16th. I had two or three good seasons towards the close of the week. Last night I believe I grieved the Spirit by idle conversation, but this morning on my knees I have again enjoyed access to the throne. I have been pleading the promise of Christ for a baptism of the Spirit this day, 'Whatsoever ye shall ask the Father in my name, he will give it you.' This promise is absolute. Lord, increase my faith. Evening. I have had three good times, on the whole, today—two at Birstal and one at Westgate Hill. But I have to mourn over evil conversation. Lord, forgive! I have been sorely harassed with strong temptation. Lord, deliver!

"Saturday, 22nd. Of late I have had the most violent temptations and sometimes have had little heart to resist. On Thursday evening, while preaching at Birstal, my mind was fluttered and my sermon spoiled by the interruptions of a drunken man. Saw some of my old friends yesterday at Bradford. Visited one apparently dying and, in a state of nervous debility, despairing of mercy. Lord, undertake for her!

"Good Friday, 28th. On Good Friday, seventeen years since, I was awakened and converted. Help me this day, O Lord, to enter into a new covenant with thee!

"Tuesday, April 1st. On Saturday last I had a good season during the watch-night at the Heights. In that neighbourhood God is pouring out his Spirit and awakening sinners. Preached yesterday at the opening of Dudley Hill chapel. I had not much liberty. The presence of two or three preachers fettered me. When shall I be free from the fear of man?"

To Mr. Jennings he writes, the 4th of this month: "T. A. tells me you are ill; and as he intends to see you tomorrow, he wishes me to write to you by him. My time is very limited; but as a proof of my regard for you, I will just scrawl two or three lines. Your affliction is intended for good. It is sent by your own Father, and he loves you with an infinite affection. May he fill you with comfort! It is of greater importance to have a sanctified use of affliction than to be delivered out of it. 'The Lord knoweth the way that you take: when he hath tried you, you shall come forth as gold.' I heard something of your preaching. If the Lord spare you to preach again, be resolved to preach more plainly and faithfully than ever."

"Tuesday, July 8th. While speaking to the society at Birkenshaw tonight, after preaching, my soul was quickened. O for a baptism of the Spirit! I still have to mourn over my instability. The devil pursues me with horrible temptations and I do no resist as I ought. O the depths of corruption in my heart! Come, Lord Jesus, and create all things new!

"Wednesday, 9th. I have had a good season this evening at Gildersome Street. But I want to live every moment through the day in the Spirit. O for the power of love!

"Friday, 11th. I have been much profited in reading *The Life of Mrs. Rogers*. She excels in describing the simplicity of faith. I do believe in Christ. I give myself to him. Lord, take all! I had but a barren season at Batley tonight.

"Tuesday, 15th. What is my present state? I have faith in God and love to God. I feel a reliance on Christ as my Saviour. I have desires after perfect love. I am seeking for it. I strive to believe for it. I feel power, in some degree, to maintain the spirit of prayer through the day. I have been learning of late more clearly to distinguish between temptation and sin. Where the *will* does not consent to evil there is no sin. I have heard today that two persons were awakened when I was last at Haworth, and that one was awakened last Friday evening at Batley. Lord, the work is thine: take all the glory!

"Thursday, 24th. Much discouraged. The congregation at Birstal is small. Can it be the will of the Lord that I should remain here another year! I have been variously exercised this week. I want this perfect love. Lord, send it!"

The severe afflictions of Mr. Stoner's excellent mother were about this time terminated.[1] She had endured them as a Christian. Her friends cherish in affectionate remembrance the many pleasing proofs which she afforded of peaceful conformity to the will of her heavenly Father, and of a scriptural meetness for the "inheritance of the saints in light." Mr. Stoner records her death in the following affecting terms:

"August 11th. My dear mother is gone, gone to heaven! After a long, excruciating illness she has left the sorrows of the world. Her sufferings under the gnawings of a cancer in the breast for nearly two years were unknown to all but herself and her God. But now her pain is over for ever. She is before the throne! Her loss will be keenly felt.

---

1   A brief notice of her experience, character, and happy death, appeared in the *Wesleyan-Methodist Magazine* for 1824, pp. 140, 141.

She has been an affectionate and diligent wife, a true helper, and a kind and tender mother. Her charities, for her situation, have been great. I have lost the best human friend I ever had. But her sufferings were so exceedingly great that my sorrow for her departure is mingled with joy and gratitude to God that she is gone. I saw her for the last time on Wednesday evening, and on Sunday afternoon at about five o'clock she died.

> Her languishing head is at rest,
>   Its thinking and aching are o'er;
> Her quiet immovable breast
>   Is heaved by affliction no more:
> Her heart is no longer the seat
>   Of trouble and torturing pain;
> It ceases to flutter and beat,
>   It never shall flutter again.

"From this hour I intend, God helping me, to begin again. What are all the vanities of the world when we look at death and eternity! Lord, sanctify this dispensation to the family, especially to ——, who is the only one of the family not in society.

"Saturday, September 27th. Glory be to God! He is mine and I am his. Last Saturday night at the band-meeting I felt my heart melted within me from a consciousness of my slackness and unfaithfulness. I gave myself to the Lord; and while Mrs. Clapham was praying, I felt the application of the Saviour's blood and believed that God had sanctified my soul. During this week I have had reasonings and strugglings, but I still believe.

"Wednesday, October 29th. I have hitherto retained, in some degree, my evidence of peace. I often have reasonings and combats on the subject, but I look to Christ; and, living by faith, I shall prevail. Lord, help me to conquer!"

Here Mr. Stoner's diary closes. Why he continued it no longer cannot now be ascertained. From his uniform temper and conduct, one thing may be safely affirmed: that his inserting no further notices of his religious experience in this interesting record did not arise from any spiritual declension. Enough, however, remains of his diary and enough has been introduced into the preceding pages to disclose the peculiar spirit of his piety—deep, humble, fervent, faithful; alive to every call of duty, keenly apprehensive of danger, and satisfied with nothing but the hallowing communications of pure and perfect love.

Of his earnestness in prayer for the prosperity of religion during his residence at Birstal, his friends retain a pleasing recollection. It seemed to pervade all his public ministrations. It often led him, between four and five o'clock in the morning, to pour out his heart in the vestry of the chapel, when no eye witnessed his fervent pleadings but the eye of him "who seeth in secret." It was particularly observable at the commencement of the Lord's days. One of the writers of these *Memoirs* went into the neighbourhood of Birstal, while Mr. Stoner was there, to preach occasional sermons, and spent the night of Saturday at Mr. Stoner's house. Early in the morning, about or before five o'clock, he was awakened by a murmuring noise in an adjoining room. On being fully roused from sleep, he ascertained that it was Mr. Stoner wrestling with God that his blessing might rest on the church and accompany the ministry of the word—that it might visit his own soul and succeed his labours that day. "Once," observes Mr. Gilpin, "in a love-feast at Gildersome, I remember his praying six or seven different times for the blessing of God and the outpouring of the Holy Spirit. His whole soul was absorbed in the work. Self appeared to be annihilated and the glory of God in the salvation of men to be all in all." It is not surprising that one who thus lived in the spirit of prayer and humble dependence on God should have great fruit in his public labours.

In the Birstal Circuit, as well as in his other stations, he paid much attention to prayer-meetings. It was while here that he published the following rules for the proper management of such meetings. To some it may appear that the time allotted to each prayer is too short; but upon the whole, the regulations suggested are deserving of much attention.

Prayer-Meetings

Prayer-meetings, when properly conducted, are useful and necessary auxiliaries to the preaching of the gospel. But it is feared their usefulness is, in many cases, greatly prevented by various errors connected with the conducting of them. For the removal of these errors, the following rules are recommended:

1. Begin the meeting *precisely* at the time appointed.

2. Let the meeting be opened by singing two or three verses; and afterwards let not more than one verse, or two short ones, be sung at a time.

3. Let every prayer leader have his memory stored with a variety of suitable verses of hymns, that there may be no necessity to have recourse to a book after the meeting is commenced.

4. Let the tune be suited to the hymn. For solemn subjects, let the tune be *grave*, but not *drawling;* for cheerful subjects, let the singing be *lively*, but not *light*.

5. Let the person who opens the meeting pray for the sick, the dying, the king, the nation, the world, etc. And on *ordinary* occasions, let this suffice. Let others pray for a *present* baptism of the Holy Ghost.

6. If anyone give a word of exhortation, let him not exceed from five to ten minutes.

7. Let no individual pray long. *In general*, the utmost limit ought to be about two minutes. It will be found much better for one person to pray twice or thrice in the course of the meeting than to pray once a long time. *Long* praying is, in general, both a *symptom* and a *cause* of spiritual deadness. If you cannot pray short, be silent.

8. Let no time be lost. If *one* person *will* not, let another begin. Two or three, at least, should pray between the times of singing.

9. While one is praying, let all others be silent, except at the close of a petition; then, *"let all the people say, Amen"* (Psa. 106:48).

10. Let not the meeting exceed an hour.

Pray with *humility*. Remember, you are *sinners* approaching a God of infinite holiness.

Pray with *simplicity*. What! will you attempt to captivate the ear of the Almighty by elegant sentences and high-sounding diction? "Be not rash with thy mouth, and let not thine heart be hasty to utter anything before God: for God is in heaven, and thou upon earth: therefore let thy words be few" (Eccles. 5:2).

Pray with *earnestness*. "And he said, I will not let thee go, except thou bless me" (Gen. 32:26).

Pray in *the name of Christ*. "Whatsoever ye shall ask the Father in my name, he will give it you" (John 16:23).

Pray in *faith*. "What things soever ye desire, when ye pray, believe that ye receive them, and ye shall have them" (Mark 11:24).

Hitherto Mr. Stoner had been exercised by the temptations of Satan, the infirmities of his own nature, and the ordinary oppositions of the world, but he had not partaken largely of the bitter cup of domestic affliction. The death of his mother appears to have been the first serious breach that was made in his family connexions. From this period, however, as the succeeding chapter will declare, he was painfully visited by this class of human sufferings. To prepare him for his early removal, it seemed good to his heavenly Father to examine and perfect his Christian virtues by every species of trial. Nor did he "faint in the day of adversity." The spiritual excellencies which had adorned the preceding stages of his earthly pilgrimage continued to shine with mild and undiminished lustre amid the dreary scenes of that dark valley which he was at length called to traverse. He endured the trial. Relying on the arm of omnipotence, he was elevated above the changes, sorrows, and privations of time; he could meekly rejoice in prospect of the "divine and ineffable fruits of immortality," and could apply to his personal condition that cheering description of the saint's progress to the heavenly Jerusalem, on which he had often expatiated with delight in his public ministrations, "Blessed is the man whose strength is in thee; in whose heart are the ways of them. Who passing through the valley of Baca make it a well; the rain also filleth the pools. They go from strength to strength, every one of them in Zion appeared before God."

8

Ministry at York

He receives an appointment to the York Circuit—The discussion which took place in Conference on this subject—He has two severe attacks of sickness—Extract from a letter to Miss Milnes—Death of his daughter—Extract from a letter to Mr. William Parkin—Death and character of Mrs. Stoner—Under these painful bereavements, he strives to allay his grief by engaging zealously in the discharge of his official duties—His labours and success—Various extracts from his correspondence—His second marriage—Other extracts — He promotes the erection of a third chapel at York—General remarks on his experience and views during his residence in that city.

For several reasons it appeared desirable, both to Mr. Stoner and the societies in the Birstal Circuit, that he should continue among them a third year. He had secured their esteem and attachment; he was in the very height of his usefulness and, in conjunction with some active and influential friends, was projecting new plans which promised, if accompanied by the blessing of God, very considerably to extend the influence of religion in the vicinity of Birstal. The Conference, however, after having carefully examined the subject, judged it proper that he should remove to York, to which city he was accordingly appointed. Here his highly-valued colleagues were the Rev. John Slack and the Rev. Dr. McAllum, with whom he laboured for two years in great unanimity and peace.

It may not be improper to record that the question of his removal from Birstal excited much discussion in the Conference. Not a few of the preachers, considering the peculiar circumstances and feelings of the Birstal societies, and apprehensive of the consequences which might possibly arise from the disappointment of their hopes, pleaded strongly for his continuance among them; while others, adverting to the claims and wants of the York Circuit, urged with equal earnestness that he should be appointed to that important station. During this debate Mr. Stoner was present, and to him it was sufficiently painful and embarrassing. His nature shrank from the exposure to which he was subjected, and his insuperable diffidence prevented him from expressing any sentiments of his own on the subject in the presence of so large an assembly of his brethren. He deemed it most consistent with his age and character to resign himself in silence to the presiding control of heaven and submissively await the decision of judgments more mature than his own. The point was at length settled by a majority of votes. One argument which had been chiefly employed in favour of his remaining at Birstal arose from his late usefulness there. When the debate was terminated he addressed a note to the secretary, modestly disclaiming the honour which had been attributed to him, and expressing his persuasion that the religious prosperity of the Birstal Circuit ought mainly to be ascribed, under God, to the zealous and faithful exertions of his venerated superintendent, Mr. Nelson. The watchful discipline to which, as different parts of his diary amply testify, he had submitted in the investigation of his motives, was not in vain. From the above-mentioned incident it is evident that he had successfully learned "in lowliness of mind to esteem others better than himself," and to rejoice in the diffusion of evangelical light and blessing by the instrumentality of others, though his own name were unrewarded and forgotten.

The close confinement of this Conference, which was held, during a sultry season, in the Old chapel at Leeds, appears to have had an unfriendly effect on his health; and the day after his return to Birstal, he was seized with a violent attack of cholera morbus, a disease at that time extensively and fatally prevalent. For some days his life was in imminent danger; nor could he, until after a lapse of more than three weeks, recover strength sufficient to enable him to remove to his new Circuit. Here, however, he arrived in the beginning of September, 1824, much wasted and debilitated but anxious to engage in his wonted labours.

He soon found himself among a people differing in several respects from those whom he had left but partaking, in an encouraging degree, of "the spirit of grace and of supplications." Many prayers had been offered at York, during the sittings of Conference, for a richer communication of heavenly influence, and many tokens and pledges of prosperity had been received. All this was very cheering to the mind of Mr. Stoner. He entered upon his duties with his usual ardour, but was again interrupted in his proceedings by indisposition. The Circuit was at that time a very laborious one, embracing almost the whole of what are now the York and Tadcaster Circuits. It appears that the three preachers regularly visited nearly fifty villages within a compass of ten miles round York, and in one direction rode fifteen miles. This was, at first, too much for Mr. Stoner; and in consequence of the delicate state of his health and his frequent exposure to the night air, he contracted a severe cold on his throat and lungs which rendered it necessary that he should again desist, for upwards of a fortnight, from his public duties.

When he was recovering he wrote to Miss Milnes, of Bradford, then at a boarding school in Leeds, as follows: "'Wherefore should a living man complain?' I am sure that I, of all men, have no reason to complain, except of myself. My heavenly Father has been always kind to me—O how kind! And I have been unfaithful to him—O how unfaithful! He has blessed me all my life long and he still blesses. If he has afflicted, it has been gently and slightly and in much love; and now he is restoring me to health. I preached twice in York on Sunday, and again last night; and now I feel better and stronger than I have done since I left Birstal. Praise the Lord! And now, my dear Eliza, live to God. What a mercy that he has drawn your heart after himself in your tender years! O devote yourself entirely to his service! Remember there is no happiness to be found anywhere else, and happiness is the object of universal pursuit. What crowds are seeking it in dress, in amusements, in mirth, in company, in anything but religion! Poor, gay, empty, fluttering, painted butterflies! And are these the souls for whom Christ shed his heart's blood? And are these to live for *ever?*—to live, either mingling their groans among the shrieks of the damned in hell, or joining in the chorus of angels and saints in heaven through an *unwasting eternity?* O eternity, eternity! who can tell the length of eternity? And this eternity is *yours*. O *live* for it! Never, never omit the duty of prayer. However backward and listless you may sometimes feel towards this duty, always be determined to break through. Never give way to temptation in the omission of *this* duty. It is your life. 'Continue instant in prayer,' and watch against everything that would lead you astray. May God bless you! Avoid trifling conversation. Try sometimes to drop a word for God. Who knows how useful you may be to some of the young ladies around you?"

Scarcely was Mr. Stoner's health re-established when he was called to pass through distressing scenes of domestic affliction and bereavement. His only daughter, a lovely and promising child, was first affected with symptoms of water in the head, and afterwards seized with the hooping-cough, accompanied, it would seem, with scarlet-fever. He had a very tender affection for her and discovered much solicitude for her recovery, mingled, however, with a spirit of meek submission to his heavenly Father's will. Every means was assiduously employed, but in vain. She died on the 25th of October, soon to be followed by another whose loss was far more deeply and painfully felt.

To the affliction of his family, the death of his daughter, and the alarming situation of Mrs. Stoner, he refers in the following extract from a letter to Mr. W. Parkin of Hightown near Birstal, dated November 3rd: "Since we came to this city we have seen much affliction. Scarcely has a day passed without more or less suffering, either of parents or children. Soon after our arrival I caught a severe cold and was laid aside for some time; but thanks to the Giver of every blessing, he has raised me again. I have now been above a month in my regular work and am at present tolerably well. One of our little boys was taken ill, but he soon recovered. Our little daughter was then seized and threatened with water on the brain. By this she was much reduced in strength, and then caught the hooping-cough, which, with teething and our close situation combined, brought a termination to her earthly course on Monday morning before last. The day after we had interred our lovely Louisa, my wife was delivered of a dead daughter. This was caused, I believe, by exertion of body and anxiety of mind. Since the time of her confinement, she has been very ill. She is still so at the present time; and if she recover, which I hope will be the case, it is probable from her situation that her recovery will be tedious and slow. But shall I complain and murmur? No. I dare not. I know what I have deserved—everlasting damnation. And all above this is rich mercy. And O! what numberless mercies I still enjoy! May God make me thankful! I dare not murmur, because I know it is the Lord's doing; and he is too wise to do wrong and too good to be unkind. 'Whom the Lord loveth, he chasteneth;' and though this 'chastening for the present seemeth not to be joyous, but grievous,' it is intended hereafter to yield the 'peaceable fruit of righteousness.' I dare not murmur, because when the Almighty tried me with health, and ease, and comfort, I did not make the improvement which I ought to have done; so now he has taken the rod into his hand and put me into the school of affliction. But O my stubborn heart! How dull and unteachable am I! May God help me to learn the lessons of his grace! I dare not murmur, because I know that the 'sufferings of this present time are not worthy to be compared with the glory which shall be revealed in us,' if we are but faithful to the grace of God. I am greatly gratified and encouraged to find that you remember me at the throne of grace.'

> All the promises are sure
> To persevering prayer.

I earnestly request you still to plead for me that God would bless me and make me a blessing. Be assured I do not forget you; but O that my prayers were more prevalent to draw down blessings on myself and others whom I endeavour to bring before the footstool of the throne. You say, 'Some weeks back my soul has not been in so lively a state.' How is this? O take care! Keep alive and lively. Keep the fire burning. Dread lukewarmness as you dread hell-fire. When anything of this kind is creeping over you, immediately take the alarm; run to the 'throne of grace' and there weep and groan and plead and wrestle till you feel that the intercourse is again open and that all is right between God and your soul. May you have eternal access to that 'tree of life, the leaves of which are for the healing of the nations!'"

The hopes which he entertained of Mrs. Stoner's recovery proved painfully delusive. Her constitution had been failing for some time and at length sank under the afflictions, domestic and personal, through which she was called to pass. Her deportment during the whole of her sickness was eminently Christian and edifying and her departure unusually calm and peaceful. She died in the 28th year of her age, just a fortnight after her beloved daughter, and was interred in the same quiet resting-place at Barwick. A funeral sermon was preached on the occasion by one of the compilers of these *Memoirs,* from Prov. 14:32: "The righteous hath hope in his death."

It is justly remarked by Dr. McAllum that "he must have been more or less than man who did not feel under these bereavements." To her husband the loss of Mrs. Stoner was incalculable. Strictly observant of his views, dispositions, and habits, she laboured in every way within her power to promote his personal comfort and ministerial usefulness; she cheerfully entered into his plans and usages, solaced him under his discouragements, and cordially united with him in prayer and other religious exercises. She was, to use his own language, "truly a help meet for him, one who was always ready to multiply his joys by joining in them, and to lighten his loads by sharing them." He could "mournfully but thankfully testify that 'she had done him good and not evil all the days of her life.'"

The following sketch of her character is extracted from a short notice by Mr. Stoner inserted in the *Wesleyan-Methodist Magazine* for 1825, pp. 356-357: "Various excellencies shone out in her character. The graces of the Spirit were implanted within, and by the fostering care of the great 'Keeper of the vineyard,' through the means of spiritual sunshine and showers and sanctified storms, these plants of the Lord's right-hand planting rose to a considerable degree of vigour and maturity. She was clothed with humility. She had low thoughts of herself, high thoughts of her Christian friends, and exalted thoughts of her great Redeemer. Her meekness and patience were exemplary. Her disposition, by nature, was gentle and kind; and this, by grace, was so mellowed and refined that her husband cannot recollect that he ever saw her angry or that he ever heard her speak a word to any one harsh or unkind. She had eminently the ornament of a meek and quiet spirit, which is in the sight of God of great price. Her industry and attention to the duties of her family were worthy of notice. In the redemption of time she was an admirable pattern.

In her the words of the wise man were fully exemplified: 'She looketh well to the ways of her household, and eateth not the bread of idleness.' She loved the Word of God. The New Testament was her constant pocket companion. She read the Bible regularly through once a year and read it much upon her knees."

Deprived of such a conjugal associate, Mr. Stoner found his situation truly mournful and desolate. Two children indeed remained, dear remembrancers of departed excellence; yet they served not always to allay, but often to re-awaken and augment, his sorrows. For a short season he seemed in danger of falling under the influence of deep mental depression. He betook himself, however, to the duties of his closet and of his ministerial office; he received every mark of kind and sympathizing attention from the friends at York; and he shortly had the comfort to feel that his anguish was considerably alleviated, though the wound remained.

To the engagements of the pulpit, both regular and occasional, he devoted himself, if possible, with an increase of zeal and diligence. His labours were, as usual, eminently acceptable and useful. At some seasons the energy of his remonstrances and appeals was irresistible. Once, as he himself informed Mr. Jennings, he was preaching an occasional charity sermon in the vicinity of York and observed that he did not remember ever to have beheld so deep and general an influence resting on a congregation as he witnessed that day. In the course of his sermon a little boy began to weep bitterly. A person in the same pew inquired what was amiss—if he wished to go out. "No," replied the child. "But I will *never say foul words any more.*" An incident like this may seem trivial, but it illustrates the peculiar *point* and *force* of Mr. Stoner's pulpit addresses. He could not satisfy himself with general declamations, how ardent soever they might be, against sin and in recommendation of holiness. He descended to particulars. He selected *characters* and *cases*. He strove to impress conviction on *every* heart, and by the accompanying demonstration and power of the divine Spirit, often succeeded in flashing illumination through the most ignorant and untutored mind, and in rousing the most inattentive to trembling inquiry and penitent resolution.

During his residence at York, he bestowed much attention on the management of prayer-meetings. It is in reference to his proceedings at this period and in this particular that Dr. McAllum remarks, "At the close of almost every evening service, whether in town or country, he held a prayer-meeting; and without calling on any one by name, he left those to engage who felt disposed, only cautioning all against 'much speaking' and 'vain repetitions.' The prayer of the petitioners was for a present blessing, for a spirit of conviction to wound and the healings of the balm of Gilead to save the soul. He never suffered more than one to engage at the same time in audible prayer. He disliked noise for its own sake; and being desirous that everything should be done 'decently and in order,' and that our 'good should not be evil spoken of,' he could not endure any one to stamp with the foot or strike a table or form with the hand—a practice, he thought, which, if it did not come of evil, did not tend to good. If any persons were in distress, he spoke to the individuals softly and encouragingly while another was engaged in public prayer; but he preferred dismissing the company, that he might remain alone with the convinced souls; or, at most, that only two or three might continue with him and them; and then he would wrestle in prayer till the contrite spirits found 'redemption in the blood of Christ, the forgiveness of sins.'"

He paid much regard also to band-meetings and endeavoured, in conjunction with his excellent colleagues, to promote their establishment. "The public band-meeting in York," says Dr. McAllum, "was revived; and it proved, and continues to prove, eminently a means of grace. It was one which Mr. Stoner was careful to attend, and not without advantage to himself and much to the benefit of others. Ready and prompt of speech for the Lord as he was, I sometimes thought him unnecessarily disposed to be grieved with the pauses in the meeting; but few could retire from the assembly without finding their minds quickened and enlivened."

The labours of himself and valuable coadjutors were crowned with an encouraging measure of success. Dr. McAllum testifies that "a multitude both of men and women believed, a great proportion of whom continue to hold fast their confidence. At least four hundred persons were added unto the Lord; and though not exclusively by his instrumentality, yet he was an eminent instrument in the good which was done. His calls to other Circuits on public occasions were frequent and urgent, and he could not resist them all; but his absence was felt to be a loss which was very imperfectly compensated by the benefits of his visits elsewhere."

The York Circuit was divided in the year 1825. This division, as Dr. McAllum proceeds to observe, "was in every respect an advantage to York and secured the better attendance of the preachers to their appointments within its bounds. The second year, the one, if possible, of more diligent and certainly of less interrupted labour, was not distinguished by much increase. But the work deepened remarkably. Believers were blessed with the abiding witness of their adoption; they were established in the faith, rooted and grounded in love."

To trace the different workings of Mr. Stoner's mind during the period of his continuance at York would undoubtedly be interesting and edifying, but materials fail. The writers must therefore satisfy themselves by introducing such extracts from his letters as appear most proper to unfold his unaltered principles and consistent aims.

To Miss Milnes he writes, December 6th, 1824, about a month after Mrs. Stoner's death: "It gives me great pleasure to hear of your welfare—that you are still walking in religion's ways and determined to persevere. O may the God of all grace inspire you with wisdom and resolution, that you may be enabled to avoid every snare and conquer every temptation! The Lord has called me to pass through deep waters since I came to York, but hitherto he has helped me. It is the Lord, and I know he cannot do wrong. I have lost the flower of all my earthly blessings, but my loss is her eternal gain. Nearly her last words were, 'The—Lord—is—my salvation!' Let you and me be determined so to live that in our last, *honest* hour we also may triumph in the Lord as our salvation. Praise the Lord, I am much better in bodily health now than I have been before since I came to York. I have been a fortnight in my regular work and hope I shall be able, with the blessing of the Lord, to persevere. And now, my dear Eliza, watch and pray. O live to God! The world around us is perishing and vanishing. We are hastening to eternity. Strange that we should be so indifferent to its all-important concerns! I hope at last you will meet in heaven that unworthy servant of Christ, David Stoner. P.S. The motto on your seal touched my heart: 'Today we bloom, tomorrow die.' O how true! 'Be ye also ready.'"

On the 16th of August, 1825, he wrote to Mr. Jennings, who was just then received as a probationer in the Wesleyan itinerancy: "I looked over the stations for your name and found a Joseph Jennings, which I suppose was intended for you. I congratulate you upon your introduction among a body of men equal to whom, I believe, you will not find another in the Lord's world. I congratulate you upon your now being called to consecrate all your bodily and intellectual powers to the most important, the most honourable, and yet the most responsible work in the world—the work of saving souls from death, of spreading the knowledge of the Saviour's name, of thinning the ranks of the devil's army, of increasing at once the joy and the population of heaven. May God give you great success! 'Hope for the best and prepare for the worst' is an old proverb well worthy of attention.

"You have, I believe, the right object in view—the glory of God in the salvation of souls. I hope you will always keep it in view. For this you must labour, and study, and preach, and pray, and read, and travel. Nothing *less* and nothing *else* than this must satisfy you. To preach fine sermons, to acquire learning, to gain admiration and popularity are despicable objects when compared with the salvation of souls. 'Let thine eye be single!'"

He then cautions his young friend against imitating those who strive to be *great* rather than *useful* preachers and advises him to follow such for his model as are seeking to be *"good* preachers."

"To be useful," he proceeds, "is the motive which sets them to work and keeps them at it. They labour to gain learning and the best gifts; to acquire the best language, the best ideas, the best figures, and the best action; yet they sacrifice all on this altar—to gain the salvation of souls. The plainness, simplicity, faithfulness, and energy which characterized the ministry of the first Methodist preachers are the objects of their imitation. They endeavour to 'declare the *whole counsel* of God.' They do not forget to preach to *sinners* and to preach to them *as sinners*—sinners on the verge of ruin, dancing over the precipice of perdition, just dropping into hell. They still remember that all means are vain without a divine influence, and therefore they pray, and excite others to pray, for the outpourings of the Spirit. United, persevering prayer is heard and answered. The fountains of the great deep are broken up. Floods of grace descend, and sinners are converted to God.

"As soon as you have got comfortably into your Circuit, you must send me a particular account of your proceedings and prospects. Of course, you will have learned before now that Methodism is a *very* different thing in the south from what it is in Yorkshire. I would advise you, if possible, to transplant Yorkshire Methodism into Oxfordshire and Buckinghamshire; but go about your work mildly and gently, though resolutely and steadily. Don't be hot-headed, rash, and overbearing. You must *draw* and not *drive*. First, gain the affections of the people. This perhaps you may do in six months; then the other six, you may do almost what you will with them.

"The Lord is still carrying on his work in a small degree among us. But we want a mighty flood. Seldom a week passes over but more or fewer souls enter into liberty; and if this is the case *in summer*, we hope to have a great ingathering in *winter*. 'If you wish to see extraordinary *effects* you must use extraordinary *efforts*.' This is a maxim confirmed by Scripture and the experience of the church in all ages. Take it and act upon it. In your next, send me word what course of study you are pursuing. You must now begin to work as you have never done. Be determined to be a workman, a *labourer*, and not *a loiterer*. May the Lord bless you!"

To Miss Mary Ann Rhodes of Birstal, afterwards his wife, and now his sorrowing widow, he writes, under the date of October 28th, the same year: "It is now near midnight. All around me is still—silent as death! Methinks many angels are here, and some of my friends from the heavenly world! How solemn! How delightful! The minster clock strikes! Hear it. Gone! Gone! Gone! Gone! Gone! Gone! Gone! Gone! Gone! Gone! Gone! Gone!—October 28th, 1825, is gone for ever!! What account has it carried to the recording angel?

O that we may live for eternity! Rest not without purity of heart. Be determined to get it, and then you will help me to get it. And O how much for our interest and advantage to have it! I have had it, but it is gone! surely not for ever gone! The Lord has been trying me, and I have not stood the trial. I have lost ground instead of gaining. May the Lord have mercy upon me! O help me by your prayers, and example, and influence, and exhortations, to regain my ground."

The above was evidently written during a season of depression and discouragement. It partakes of that severity in pronouncing judgment on himself which has already been observed in different extracts from his diary. He appears, however, soon to have recovered that evidence of spiritual purity without which he could not be satisfied; and during the remainder of his time at York, and more visibly, if possible, during the short term he spent at Liverpool, he afforded the strongest practical proof of its enjoyment and influence.

He had remained twelve months in the state of a widower when, after much prayer and deliberation, he entered into the marriage connexion with the person to whom the preceding letter was addressed. This union was soon and prematurely dissolved by the hand of death, but during its continuance it appears to have been a source of great mutual enjoyment to himself and to her who now survives to cherish the recollection of his virtues and mourn over his early and unexpected removal.

January 7th and 9th, 1826, he writes to Mr. Jennings: "From the wickedness which prevails in your neighbourhood, and the general dullness and deadness of your religious societies, perhaps you will be tempted to impatience—especially from the latter. You must guard against that danger. Nothing is to be gained by driving and scolding. Everything almost may be done by *drawing* and *melting* and *winning*. If the people will not pray as fast and loud and short; or if they will not say Amen as you wish them to do—still be gentle and patient. *Creep* first—then *walk*—then run—and last of all *fly*. But at the same time keep your own soul alive to God. Let the fire be always burning brightly and ardently on your own altar, wherever it may blaze or blink beside. And how this is to be done you know—by prayer and praise and faith and watchfulness. I hope you have got over most of your fears by this time. What have you to fear, man? He who fears God needs have no other fear. Preach on, and pray on, and praise on, and believe on; and fear not.

"It appears you have plenty of walking and preaching, and a fine field for usefulness. Labour on, and expect to see fruit. Let nothing else content you. I have just been at our band-meeting. Praise the Lord! He has blessed and filled my soul. I felt my cup to run over.

> What a mercy is this, what a heaven of bliss!
> How unspeakably happy am I!
> Gather'd into the fold, with thy people enroll'd,
> With thy people to live and to die!

"You will have heard, I dare say, that I am married again. I can live to God better in a married than in a single state, and it is my intention to live to him. May he help me! We are not getting on so well in our Circuit as we did last year at this time. We had very little increase the last quarter—only about half a dozen, and about fifty on trial. But praise the Lord for half a dozen! We are praying and looking and longing—surely the shower will come.

"9th. I had a pretty good day yesterday. One young man cried for mercy in the prayer-meeting and obtained liberty. Praise the Lord for *one!* But I want thousands. It is my daily prayer, 'Lord, lay on my heart the burden of souls! Let me feel for souls! Give me souls!' And surely the Lord will answer prayer. Pray for me, and pray on until prayer is lost in praise in the light and glory of heaven. May God bring us thither!"

The following is an extract from two letters addressed, February 4th and 13th of the same year, to his sisters-in-law, Misses Lena and Jane Rhodes of Birstal: "Such is this vain world! Happy they whose treasure and hearts are above the stars! O my girls, 'set your affections on things above, not on things on the earth.' I hope we are creeping on a little in our society at York, but not so swiftly as our expectations and wishes. Pray for us, that we may soon have a copious shower. You must endeavour to improve your time. Whatever others do, I hope my two sisters are resolved to be women of God. You have a fine opportunity of getting a clearer knowledge of your own hearts and of the excellency, ability, and willingness of the Saviour. May the Lord help you to use it! He has been visiting you with slight affliction. May it be sanctified to your good. We have deserved everlasting *misery,* but God chastises in *mercy.*"

In a letter to Mr. Jennings under the date of March 29th he has some very useful observations. It may not be superfluous to remark that in the following extract he evidently uses the word *joy* to denote the occasional hilarity of the Christian's spirit rather than its calm and settled felicity. By the term joy, the Scriptures, it is thought, more generally designate the latter, and encourage us to believe that, in the possession of present blessings and the prospect of those scenes of future happiness which expand themselves to the eye of faith and hope, we may *habitually rejoice,* though the more sensible emotions of our joy will be subject to frequent variations.

"You complain of the want of *peace* and *joy*. As to *peace,* I need not tell you that it is our duty and privilege always to have this blessing. When justified by faith, we have *peace.* You give way to over-anxiety and fleshly reasonings about this and that and thus rob yourself of comfort. Why shall you be such an enemy to yourself? As to *joy,* it is quite another thing. No spiritual sensation of the Christian is so variable as *joy*. Sometimes there is a *'need'* for our being in *'heaviness* through manifold temptations.' Our feelings as to *joy* often depend on the state of the atmosphere, the health of the body, or the tone of the animal spirits. Don't rob yourself of *peace* by complaining that you have not sufficient *joy. Strive to* 'rejoice evermore.'

"I am glad to hear that you have a little prosperity in your Circuit. Prosperity, be it ever so little, is cause for gratitude and joy. Remember the value of *one* soul, and labour on. You still talk of your fears, and of going home. I say, Go home if you dare. If you wish to gratify the devil and displease God, *go home.* If you wish to have the curse of God upon your body and soul and all you set your hand to, *go home.* If you wish to be miserable in this world and lost in the next, *go home.* You ask, 'Is not this one proof that I am not called of God to the work—that I have not greater liberty in composing sermons, and a freedom from such distressing perplexity?' If *experience, my own* experience, and the experience of *others* is any criterion, I answer, No! I had, as I have often told you before, similar fears and perplexities; yet I have now no doubt of my call to the ministry of the gospel. Others, I see from biographical accounts, as well as hear from living witnesses, have been exercised in the same way. 'There hath no temptation taken you but such as is common to man' in the same circumstances. After a while, I have no doubt, you will rise above them. Only persevere in *prayer* and *labour*, and the sky will clear and the sun will shine."

To a young man then engaged as an assistant in a public seminary who was under the influence of much nervous debility, and among other things suffered considerable disquietude on the subject of his attempting the Christian ministry, he addressed the following pertinent and discreet remarks: "You complain that your nervous disorder has gained ground and that your memory is shattered and impaired. Now certainly, from what I learn, you can expect little else but a disordered imagination and an impaired memory. If I am rightly informed, you sit up late at night, *even* sometimes past midnight. Then of course, instead of being up early in the morning and taking an invigorating walk, you are dozing in bed; and as nature must have her proper quantity of repose, you are under the necessity of sleeping between school hours. Such a plan as this, with your sedentary employment, would be enough to ruin a *good* constitution and to produce depression with all its accompanying evils; of making molehills into mountains and filling the mind with *real* agony, though arising from *imaginary* causes. Now, my dear youth, you must change your plan. Remember the old adage, which is not to be despised *because* it is *old*:

> Early to bed, and early to rise,
> Will make a man healthy, wealthy, and wise.

You must deny yourself and go to bed in good time. Deny yourself of the 'lust of finishing' as it has been called. Fix your hour; and when the hour arrives, if it find you in the midst of a sentence or word, do not finish, but retire to rest. In the morning also fix your hour, and pray to God for strength to rise. When the mornings are fine, take a walk. The more time you spend in exercise in the open air when the weather is dry, consistently with your other duties, the better it will be for your body and mind. *Fasting* cannot be very proper for you in your weak state. You can *abstain* without diminishing anything from the quantity and nutrition of your food. 'Mind not high things.' I think you had better let preaching alone at present. Next to maintaining your union with God, your first care ought to be the restoration of your health. Your nervous depression, as long as it is cherished by your neglect of the right means to remove it, will prevent you from making anything out successfully in preaching. I would advise you to lay aside all thoughts on that subject for a short time. My dear youth, only be careful to maintain a good conscience and all will be well. Your heavenly Father will support and direct you."

During the second year of his residence at York he assiduously exerted himself in promoting the erection of a third chapel in that city. The situation which was chosen for this purpose is at a convenient distance from both the other chapels, in a much neglected neighbourhood, occupied chiefly by the lowest ranks of society. It was his settled conviction that, while the ministers of the Wesleyan Connexion are bound to promote the spiritual welfare of all who come within their reach, they have a *special* commission to the poorest and most untutored. The erection, therefore, of a suitable chapel among such a people was, as Dr. McAllum remarks, "a measure very near his heart; and but for his exhortations it would probably never have been effected." So intent was he on this project that his consent to remain a third year at York was suspended, in part, on its accomplishment. He had the satisfaction of assisting at the opening of this chapel just before his departure to his next and last station—nor were his hopes concerning it in vain. It has already been the means of extensive good in the district where it stands.

The period which Mr. Stoner spent at York, though shaded by much suffering and privation, was by no means the least beneficial of his life with regard to his own spiritual improvement. His religious experience acquired a softer and richer maturity. His views became still more abstracted from the vanities of earth and fixed on the felicities of heaven. The scenes of mortality which he witnessed in his own family were ordered in mercy. They evidently directed a larger portion of his attention to the solemnities of death and served, by the unerring appointment of divine providence, to render his mind more familiar with that awful—but not cheerless—passage to the everlasting hills of light and immortality through which he was shortly to be conducted. The "only wise God our Saviour," to whom the faithful Christian has resigned all his concerns, seldom suffers anything to take him by surprise. By the invisible agency of his grace, pressing surrounding circumstances and passing occurrences into its service, he generally gives a secret current to the thoughts, and a peculiar character to the feelings, which gradually prepare the individual for approaching events. So Mr. Stoner found it. After he had stood on the verge of that grave which folded in its dark bosom the remains of his beloved wife and offspring, he seems to have indulged more frequently than before in funeral meditations, to have anticipated the time of his own departure, and to have lived habitually under the impression of that truth which, in the beautiful language of Cowper, he recorded in the album of his friend Mr. Burdekin a short time before his departure from York:

> Like crowded forest-trees we stand,
> And some are mark'd to fall;
> The axe will smite at God's command,
> And soon shall smite us all.

9

Last Illness and Death

He unexpectedly receives an appointment to the Liverpool North Circuit—Closes his ministerial labours at York and visits two of his former stations on his way to Liverpool—The faithful admonitions which he delivered at Holmfirth—He commences his regular duties at Liverpool with his usual zeal and with hopeful prospects—His exemplary attention to private devotion—He advances very observably in the Christian life—Extracts from a letter to the Rev. John Slack—Probable occasion of his death—Sketch of his last sermon, with extracts from it—Extracts from a letter to the Rev. Joseph Jennings—The severity of his last illness, his deportment under it, and his truly Christian death—Circumstance of his funeral—Reflections.

During the Conference which assembled at Liverpool in 1826, which Mr. Stoner attended in virtue of his office as one of the secretaries to the Contingent Fund, he again became the unwilling subject of a discussion similar to that which had issued in his removal from Birstal. Vigorous efforts were used to procure his appointment to Liverpool, and these efforts proved ultimately successful. To the friends at York, among whom he had explicitly consented to remain a third year, this was perfectly unexpected. They felt themselves painfully disappointed, and deemed it proper to employ every respectful and constitutional means to secure his return; but considering the special circumstances and demands of Liverpool, and relying on the impartial judgment of the assembled preachers, they at length acquiesced, with much Christian temper, in the decision of Conference. To Liverpool North, therefore, Mr. Stoner was appointed, with the Rev. Robert Martin and the Rev. Edward Usher; and here, after the lapse of a few weeks, he closed his honourable course of labour and usefulness. Such exertions as were urged to obtain his services, first for York and afterwards for Liverpool, forcibly evince the growing estimation in which he was held by the Wesleyan Connexion; while the peculiarity of these cases will excuse, if they do not entirely justify, the conduct which was pursued. Such cases, however, cannot with any propriety become precedents; nor ought they to be cited by persons, whether official or otherwise, who may be tempted to allure a preacher from a station to which he is pledged, or to use any unwarrantable influence for the accommodation of their own Circuits at the expense and injury of others.

On Mr. Stoner's return from Conference he began to make preparations for his departure from York but was retarded for a while by the serious indisposition of Mrs. Stoner. At length, however, he terminated his ministerial labours at York for ever by preaching on the 27th of August, at the opening of St. George's chapel, to the completion of which he had looked forward with so much pleasure and hope.

On his way to Liverpool he preached with peculiar zeal and faithfulness at Birstal, Holmfirth, and Batley. He also attended the Missionary Anniversary at Birstal on the 30th of August—a day on which the writers of these sheets had the satisfaction of meeting with him, little thinking that they should see him no more until the resurrection of the just.

At Holmfirth he spent Sunday, September 3rd, and preached three times. In the last sermon, he so fully delivered his soul in his message that many of his hearers said at the time he had preached another farewell sermon. His last appeal to them was like the appeal of a "dying man to dying men," when, with his peculiar solemnity of look and with the deepest and strongest intonation of his voice, he exclaimed, "I charge you all to meet me at the right hand of God! Should I never see your faces again, I am 'pure from the blood' of you all! I charge you to meet me at the right hand of God!" The impression produced upon the congregation was very powerful; and it is hoped that many who heard him then, and who now know that they must hear him no more, will faithfully treasure up in their hearts his parting admonitions.

On the 7th of September he opened his regular commission at Liverpool by preaching in the evening of that day at Brunswick Chapel. He was now in a situation which differed widely from any which he had occupied in the West Riding of Yorkshire, and perhaps he felt the disadvantage of having been confined so long to one limited section of ministerial labour. His habits were formed, and it seemed to require some time before he could fully accommodate himself to the manners and customs of the people among whom he was placed. For a short season his timid spirit suffered acutely, but he soon begun to cherish the kindlier feelings of home-attachment. He was received with grateful esteem and affection, and in the different exercises of his function engaged with all his heart. He encouraged the band-meeting. He promoted preaching in private houses. He urged the importance of united prayer for richer effusions of divine influence. And in his public ministrations he poured out all his soul in earnest and affectionate entreaty. Twenty-six times he preached in Liverpool and its vicinity, and it is said that under every sermon some good was done. The *visible* effect of his pulpit addresses appears to have differed, in some respects, from what it had been in his other stations. In Yorkshire it often discovered itself in powerful commotion. In Liverpool it was seen and felt in deep, silent, solemn attention. All seemed impressed by the peculiar ardour of his manner, and penetrated, for the time at least, by the omnipotent energy of the truths which he delivered.

During his short abode at Liverpool he was indefatigably attentive to his private duties and specially observant of the sacred hours of morning devotion. He constantly rose at five o'clock and spent from an hour to an hour and a half in fervent prayer. He would then rise from his knees and sing that verse:

> Praise God from whom all blessings flow,
> Praise him, all creatures here below;
> Praise him above, ye heavenly host,
> Praise Father, Son, and Holy Ghost.

Then again he would "bow his knees unto the Father of our Lord Jesus Christ, of whom the whole family in heaven and earth is named," and wrestle in prayer for the church, for the world, and for himself, until seven o'clock. He would afterwards retire into his study and engage in exercises proper for the place until eight o'clock, at which time he came down to breakfast. Thus was he prepared to pass with calm, unembarrassed, and devout feeling through all the duties of the day.

At this period, too, he diligently maintained a practice which he had generally pursued in his other stations, and particularly, it would appear, at York—that of spending a part of every Sunday evening, after the public services of the day were concluded, with Mrs. Stoner and their servant, who was a pious young woman, in special prayer and intercession for the prosperity of the word which had been spoken that day—for the revival and extension of religion within the sphere of his personal exertions—and for a larger communication of divine grace to the church in all its denominations and the world in all its tribes. These were often seasons of peculiar profit, sealing the labours of the day with fresh exercises of piety and more lively apprehensions of the divine benignity.

In general he was about this time unusually copious and fervent in his family devotions, often dwelling with peculiar emphasis on the solemnities of death and eternity. For some weeks indeed previous to his death, all his Christian graces seemed fast ripening into their full maturity. His abstraction from the world, his union and fellowship with God, his ardent breathings after spiritual and heavenly enjoyments, particularly engaged the attention of his most intimate friends. They could not refrain from thinking that he was preparing for some great event, though they little supposed it would be that which they were soon called to mourn.

Shortly after his arrival at Liverpool, Mrs. Slack, the wife of his late excellent superintendent, died. He wrote to Dr. McAllum on the 20th of September and was then in vigorous health. By the same post he also addressed a letter of affectionate condolence to Mr. Slack, from which the following is an extract:

"I have just heard the melancholy news of the afflictive dispensation with which the Lord of all has been pleased to visit you. Great indeed is your loss, and great is the loss to your family. I sympathize with you and can mourn with them that mourn. It brings afresh to my mind recollections of sorrowful days through which I was called to pass, and in which you kindly sympathized with me. May

God be your comforter and stay! The loss to you is irreparable, but what a mercy to know that to the departed it is unutterable gain! It is the *best of all blessings* to die well and get safely home to heaven. This blessing she has attained. Danger is over. Her race is happily concluded. She has won the victory. She has received the crown. But how little we know of heaven!

> O speak, ye happy spirits! Ye alone can tell
> The wonders of the beatific sight!
> When from the bright unclouded face of God
> Ye drink full draughts of bliss and endless joy,
> And plunge yourselves in life's immortal fount.

"I doubt not but your departed wife and mine have before now renewed their acquaintance in heaven and talked over many of the affairs connected with the friends they have left behind. O that we may be found ready to join their blessed society whenever the arbiter of life and death shall summon us from the concerns of time! I know it is quite needless for me to point out to you sources of consolation. With these you are far better acquainted than I am. And with that comfort with which you have comforted others, may the great head of the church now abundantly replenish your own mind! Nature will feel, but it is our exalted privilege to have all the feelings of nature sanctified and blessed to our increase in holiness. By this means every drop of natural sorrow will be mingled with drops of spiritual comfort and sanctifying grace; and we, by hallowed affliction, shall thus be made more meet to be useful in the church on earth and glorious in the church above."

Ten days afterwards he wrote to his sister and, adverting to the sudden departure of Mrs. Slack, subjoined the simple and touching remark, "Little did I think when I shook hands with her that that hand was so soon to be cold in the grave!"

We are now arrived at the last month of Mr Stoner's earthly pilgrimage. On Sunday, the 8th of October, he preached at herculaneum Pottery and Seacombe, after which he re-passed the river Mersey. The evening was very cold and stormy; and not being accustomed to exposure in such a situation, perhaps he was not sufficiently apprehensive of his danger from the chilling air when inactive and not very warmly clothed. He appears to have had a constitutional tendency to disorder in the alimentary canal; and from this circumstance, as well as from the nature of his subsequent sufferings, it is not improbable that the disease which terminated his valuable life was produced on that occasion. For a few days, however, he made no complaint, but pursued his usual labours with unabated zeal.

On the evening of the 13th he preached in a private dwelling-house in Naylor Street from Luke 11:32: "The men of Nineveh shall rise up in the judgment with this generation and shall condemn it: for they repented at the preaching of Jonas; and, behold, a greater than Jonas is here." This was his last sermon. A copious outline of it has been found among his manuscripts, and as it affords a just specimen of the plainness and fidelity with which he exercised his ministry among the unawakened, and is connected so closely with his lamented death, it may not be amiss to insert a general view of its scope, with one or two extracts from its more pointed and impressive sections.

He opens his discourse with a forcible description of the divine benevolence of Jesus—a benevolence which extended to the *bodies* and especially to the *souls* of the people, and which admirably disclosed itself in his public instructions. Sometimes he endeavoured to *alarm* his hearers out of their sins by solemnly announcing the consequences of transgression; sometimes to *allure* them out of their sins by the most affectionate appeals to their hearts; sometimes by the most convincing arguments and powerful expostulations to *reason* them out of their sins; and sometimes, as in the text, to *shame* them out of their sins by comparing their evil conduct with the good conduct of others who enjoyed inferior privileges. He then argues that the words of the text, which were applied originally to the unrepenting Jews, may, on the ground of our superior advantages, be applied to the impenitent sinners of the present generation with increased force and accumulated energy. He proceeds to institute a comparison between the men of Nineveh and the impenitent sinners of his congregation, FIRST, in their *sins;* where he particularly instances *idolatry*, the principle of which he explains as consisting in the love and pursuit of any object, visible or invisible, rather than GOD: *pride, drunkenness, luxury,* and *obscenity*. He infers from the prophecies of Jonah and Nahum that such evils prevailed among the Ninevites, and forcibly states to what an alarming degree they prevail among us. He pursues the comparison, SECONDLY, in their *warnings*. Here he remarks that the warnings of the Ninevites were delivered by a fallible *man,* and he not one of the best of men; but ours are delivered by the Son of God.

Jonah was a *stranger* to the Ninevites and of a *strange religion,*but Jesus is he whose name we bear and whose religion we profess. Jonah wrought no *miracles* and possessed no *supernatural evidences* to prove the truth of his mission; but the authority of Jesus is sustained by his miracles, by the matchless purity of his life, by the supreme excellence of his doctrines, and by the exact accomplishment, in his person and work, of a long succession of prophecies; that Jonah gave the Ninevites but *one short warning* and then marched on; but Jesus gives us Sabbath after Sabbath, ordinance after ordinance, messenger after messenger, expostulation after expostulation, warning upon warning—He does everything but force us; that Jonah placed the danger of the Ninevites *at a distance,* the distance of forty days; but to us not a moment is promised beyond the present one; that Jonah predicted only a *temporal calamity,* but Jesus denounces *eternal destruction; and* that Jonah foretold the overthrow of Nineveh without any *express injunction to repent;* but Jesus *commands, promises, threatens,* does everything, in a word, with the merciful and professed design of softening our hearts into penitential feeling and humble acknowledgment.

He closes the comparison, THIRDLY, by tracing their *subsequent conduct.* The Ninevites *believed God,* but you practically *disbelieve him. They delayed not,* but you *delay. They repented,* but you remain *impenitent. They "cried mightily to God,"* but to this many of you are *strangers.* He applies the whole subject as one which teaches the *importance of believing God,* which affords the *highest possible encouragement to mourning penitents,* and which presents an *aspect the most awful* to such as *persevere in impenitence and sin.* All these topics are accompanied by apposite citations of Scripture clothed with striking illustrations, supported by powerful arguments, and pointed, in the most direct and faithful manner, to the consciences of his hearers.

"God," says he, in one part of his discourse, "has not given you so much as *forty* days. How much then has he given you? Has he given you *twenty* days? No. Before the end of *twenty days* your soul may be shrieking in hell, 'The harvest is past, the summer is ended, and we are not saved!' Has he given you *ten* days? No. Before the close of *ten* days you may be 'weeping and wailing and gnashing your teeth.' Has he given you *one* day? No. Before the conclusion of *twenty-four hours* your body may be a breathless corpse and your spirit excluded from the presence and favour and smile of God and shut up in darkness and despair, endless and hopeless. Has he given you *one hour?* No. Before the termination of *this hour* demons may drag your soul into the regions of torment. Has he given you a *single minute?* No. Before the expiration of *another minute* the frail machine may cease to move and your spirit be summoned to appear before God. You have no security of life. You are but tenants-at-will who may be cast out without the formality of a discharge. And yet, strange to tell! you are living in impenitence. Suppose, at the solemn hour of twelve this night, an angel were to appear to you and inform you from the God of heaven that at the end of forty days you must appear at his bar, what would be your conduct? Would you not immediately rise from your couch and cry for mercy? Would you rest day or night until you had obtained the 'knowledge of salvation by the remission of sins?' If this would be your conduct though you were sure of living *forty* days, what ought to be your conduct when you are not sure of living *one* day? By what sort of reasons can you prove that there is less need of repenting when you have *no* fixed time than there would be if you had *forty days* promised? If you were sure of living *forty* days, you would repent; but because you are not sure of living *one* day, you will not repent. Strange absurdity this! When the Ninevites had forty days set before them, they immediately repented; but you refuse to repent though you are not certain of an hour."

"Against you," he observes again, addressing the impenitent, and adverting to the *temporal* calamity which Jonah predicted to the Ninevites, "against you is denounced an *eternal* punishment—the punishment of hell. There will be the loss of heaven, the loss of happiness and hope; there will be the wrath of God, the lashes of a guilty conscience, the gnawings of unsubdued passions, the company of the miserable, the torturings of devils, the suffering of penal fire, and an assurance that these pains will be *eternal.* If the men of Nineveh repented to avoid a *few hours' pain,* what ought your conduct to be with regard to *eternal* misery? Are the arguments drawn from *eternity* less powerful than those drawn from *time?*

"*Time* is momentary duration; *eternity* is duration without end. Time is fleeting; *eternity* is stationary. *Eternity!* Reason staggers; calculation reclines her weary head; imagination is paralyzed. The minds of angels are infinitely too contracted to grasp the mighty idea of *eternity.* Yet you will not repent, though urged to it by the solemn warnings which threaten an *eternity* of woe."

In that part of his sermon where he dwells on the immediate and undelayed repentance of the Ninevites, he introduces one of those tremendous and overwhelming passages for which his ministry was sometimes remarkable. "If any inquire why we so often return with the same topics in our mouths, here they meet with an answer: it is because we have not such hearers as Jonah had. It is because you delay your repentance. We preach the necessity of repentance, the danger of the sinner, the nearness of death, the torments of eternal death, because there is need of it. If you will all repent, then like Jonah we can comparatively lay such topics aside; but until that time, these things we do preach, these things we must preach, these things we will preach, and these things we dare not do otherwise than preach. Cease to sin and we will cease to tell you that Satan is your master, that hell is your home, and eternal torment your portion. But if you still delay while our 'three days' journey' is continued, we must exclaim, Yet a few moments and you will be eternally overthrown! Yet a few moments and devils will be your tormentors! Yet a few moments and you will be enveloped in the curling, sulphurous flames of hell! Yet a few moments and your leaky, shattered bark will be launched into the stormy ocean of eternity! Hurricanes of fire and brimstone shall sweep across the infernal deep, and every blast shall howl, Eternity! Every demon you meet will shriek, Eternity! A monster shall gnaw your vitals, a monster with ten thousand tongues; and every tongue shall hiss, Eternity! Upon the gates of hell shall be written in flaming characters, 'To be opened no more through Eternity!' And will you delay your salvation any longer? Perhaps the thirty-ninth day is passing; nay, perhaps you have entered upon the fortieth. Death is whetting his scythe; nay, perhaps his dart is now entering your body! And are you still impenitent? O, like the Ninevites, delay no longer!"

During the course of this sermon, and most probably at the time that he was uttering one of the powerful paragraphs cited above, he reiterated, "Yet forty days and Nineveh shall be overthrown! Yet forty days and Nineveh shall be overthrown! Yet forty days and Nineveh shall be overthrown!" and then added, after a solemn and portentous pause, "Yet ten days and perhaps your preacher may be a lifeless corpse!" His hearers were deeply impressed; and when this faithful servant of Christ expired precisely at the end of ten days, it is not surprising if many thought that a ray of prophetic light had descended at that moment on his serious spirit and warned him of his early tomb.

In the former part of the next day, the 14th, he does not appear to have been much worse than usual. He addressed a letter to Mr. Jennings, probably the last he wrote, in which he speaks of his numerous engagements and purposes. He laments the spiritual dearth which reigned around him, but adds, "We are breaking up fresh ground. I trust we shall see good done. I feel determined, by the grace of God, to do what I can. Pray for me, that the Spirit of the Lord may descend upon the barren wilderness. Since I began this letter I have been at the children's meeting. Have you a children's meeting? If you have not, begin one. Call together the children of your congregation every Saturday afternoon to catechise them. You will find it extremely useful. I hope you are 'growing in grace' and 'knowledge.' Labour in prayer, in reading, in preaching; but do not kill yourself nor hurt yourself. You see I take the liberty of a senior to give you good advice. Good advice, if not practised to the utmost extent, is yet often useful. If it stimulate a man only to make another effort to do that which is best, it is not given in vain."

While he was at the children's meeting, mentioned in the preceding extract, he felt himself much indisposed, and shortened the service. He does not appear, however, to have been apprehensive of any immediate danger, but attended the prayer-meeting as usual in the evening. Here the malady which had secretly operated in his system for some days began to discover itself in an alarming manner. He became exceedingly ill and speedily returned home. The disease was dysentery, accompanied with strong typhoid symptoms. A surgeon's attendance was requested; and after the ordinary remedies had been tried in vain, at his suggestion a physician was called in. But all medical assistance was unavailing. The mortal hour of this exemplary minister approached, and his attendants could only mark the progress and ravages of a disease which it was not in their power to arrest.

His affliction was extremely severe. It seized him in the full vigour of manhood, at a time when his health seemed more established than it had ever been before, and it was probably irritated and increased by the vital energy with which it was opposed. His pain was deep, agonizing, and almost insupportable; but no hasty expression of murmuring or complaint ever escaped his lips. "Patience had her perfect work." By this excruciating process he was more entirely prepared for the presence of the Lord. Long had he been a "living sacrifice," sealed by the impress of the divine Spirit and consecrated on the holy altar of practical obedience; and when offered in death, he was found to be "perfect and entire, wanting nothing."

From the commencement of his illness he entertained no hope of recovery, but invariably expressed a submissive desire to "depart and be with Christ." At one time his medical attendants held a consultation on his case. After the consultation, Mrs. Stoner entered his room. "Well, Mary Ann," said he, "what is the opinion of the doctors concerning me?"

"They give but little hope concerning you," was her reply.

"What," he rejoined with evident pleasure, "then there is a chance of my getting to heaven this time."

On the 19th, upon being visited by the Rev. Messrs. Newton and Martin, he requested them not to pray for his recovery. "If," said Mr. Newton, "the Lord has work for you to do, he will raise you up."

"Mr. Newton," he replied, "my work is done!"

To Mr. Usher, who visited him with kind assiduity, he made the same request, repeating, with affecting emphasis, "My work is done!"

During the whole affliction he maintained unshaken confidence in God. To Messrs. Newton and Martin, in the interview mentioned above, he said, "I have no overflowing of joy, but peace and a strong confidence in the blood of Christ."

"The blood of Christ! the blood of Christ!" he would exclaim at intervals. "That blood has washed away your sins," said Mrs. Stoner. He replied, "I trust it has."

To Mr. Usher, who inquired if he now experienced the consolations of that religion which he had recommended to others, he said, "O yes, I do. Praise the Lord! Christ is precious. I have no ecstatic joy, but I have settled peace and strong confidence."

Amid his severe bodily sufferings it seems that he was not wholly exempted from the harassing assaults of his spiritual enemies. To these he adverted at one time when he said, "Satan tells me I shall be a castaway." These assaults, however, failed to shake his faith or impair his peace. He was also subject to occasional delirium; but, in his greatest mental wanderings, was never heard to utter an improper word—a circumstance this which affords a pleasing proof of the spirituality of his mind and the purity of his heart.

The former part of the night before he died he was in great agony. About eleven o'clock he seemed to be engaged in prayer but could not be distinctly understood. At length he was heard to say, "Praise the Lord!" and shortly afterwards, "Lord, help me! Lord, help me! Lord, undertake for me!" repeating the petitions several times; then, "Jesus, thou art my hope and confidence for ever and for ever!" After a short slumber, he awoke in extreme pain; and when it subsided, he exclaimed, "Thy blood was shed for sinners! to save sinners! 'Christ Jesus came into the world to save sinners, of whom I am chief.'" After a few minutes' pause he repeated the following lines:

> There I shall see his face,
> And never, never sin;
> There, from the rivers of his grace,
> Drink endless pleasures in.

He slumbered again, and on awaking desired to be removed from his bed. Soon after, he said, "I cannot see!" he then sank into a state of insensibility, from which he revived and asked to be replaced in bed. On being moved, he said, "I can see again!" and added, in a tender and affectionate tone, "Is she gone? Is she gone without me?" The laws of the invisible world are to us inscrutable; but it seems not irrational to suppose that, while the senses of this excellent man were closing on earthly objects, he had a mysterious perception of the presence of some departed friend—a mother perhaps, or a wife, whom he longed to accompany. He subjoined, "I fear you have brought me back to the light of this world again," and repeated,

> I nothing have, I nothing am;
> My glory's swallow'd up in shame:

but Jesus hath bled, hath died for me. 'Christ Jesus came into the world to save sinners.' Jesus, thou art my hope and confidence for ever and ever!" These were expressions which he loved to use, and they satisfactorily evince his entire reliance on the merits and mercy of his crucified Saviour.

Immediately after this, he lay for some time as if his spirit had already taken its departure. At length, however, he was perceived to breathe, but very softly, and evidently in much pain. About three o'clock in the morning he asked what was the day of the month. He was told it was Monday, October 23rd. "It will be a happy Monday for me," he replied. "I hope it will be a glorious Monday to me. I shall soon be in heaven." He again desired to rise, and experienced a recurrence of his former languor and exhaustion, attended with the convulsive efforts of expiring nature.

During the morning he had three convulsive fits in rapid succession. All around him thought that the last struggle was over. He revived, however, and called for Mrs. Stoner and his children. To Mrs. S. He said, "I have been in heaven—how is it that I have got back again hither?"

"What kind of a place is heaven?" said she.

"O, heaven is a beautiful place," was his reply.

She asked with trembling solicitude if he thought the Lord would raise him now.

"O no," said he. "It is all over!"

"What is to become of me when you are gone?"

He calmly answered, "Thy Maker is thine husband; the Lord of Hosts is his name."

He was now frequently delirious, but when recollected, his mind dwelt on divine things. "Godliness," he remarked, "is profitable unto all things."

To Mr. Usher, who took leave of him about eleven o'clock at night, he said, "Do call again. Do not leave me. Farewell! I shall meet you again at the judgment day."

The time was now come when this faithful servant of the Lord must die, and his death affords a sublime example of Christian virtue. It admirably corresponds with the tenor of his useful life. For the salvation of sinners he had lived and laboured. Solicitude for souls was the ceaseless spring of his zeal, activity, and wasting exertions. He felt the "ruling passion strong in death." He appeared to forget himself, though on the solemn verge of eternity; to forget his wife, though soon to become a disconsolate widow; to forget his two lovely boys, then passing into the sad destitution of an orphan state; but he remembered sinners. He had slumbered for some time; the silver cord seemed quite loosed and nature sinking in its last decay when, to the astonishment of every one present, he looked up and summoning all his strength to one last effort, cried aloud, "Lord! save sinners! Save them by thousands, Lord! Subdue them, Lord! Conquer them, Lord!" He reiterated these petitions nearly twenty times, then sank down, reposed his head on the pillow, and expired without a struggle or a groan, a little before twelve o'clock, aged thirty-two years, six months, and seventeen days. True soldier of the cross! "Thy years were few but full; the victim of virtue has reached the utmost goal and purpose of mortality."

The sensation which was produced by the intelligence of his death cannot easily be described. His new connexions and acquaintance in Liverpool had testified their affectionate regard during his illness by numberless calls of anxious inquiry and by fervent prayers for his recovery; but when certified of his departure, they deeply felt the loss which they had sustained, and mourned over him as a friend and brother. The feeling excited in Yorkshire was strongly marked—it was a feeling of sudden consternation, of poignant grief, and of sharp though submissive regret. In the evening of the day on which the melancholy information was conveyed to his father's house, the compilers of these pages met each other there; and though painfully familiar with the sad devastations of death, they could not but enter with peculiar emotion into the circumstances of this touching case. It was not, however, a case utterly disconsolate. The bereaved family acknowledged the hand of God, and the cheering light of pious resignation mingled itself with the dark gloom of grief. The writers found it sorrowful yet good to be there; and amid the scene which surrounded them experienced the truth of the wise man's declaration, "It is better to go to the house of mourning, than to go to the house of feasting. Sorrow is better than laughter: for by the sadness of the countenance the heart is made better."

It was intended at first to deposit his mortal remains at Barwick, where so many of his departed connexions repose. Arrangements were accordingly made to accomplish this object, but it was found to be totally impracticable. He was therefore interred on the Friday following his death in the burying ground connected with the Brunswick chapel at Liverpool. Great numbers of people attended. An appropriate and impressive address was delivered by the Rev. Robert Newton, and the funeral service was read in a very solemn and moving manner by the Rev. Robert Martin. The whole assembly was sensibly touched and softened into tears. One of the most affecting objects in the group of mourners, next to Mr. Stoner's widow and children, was his venerable father bending over the grave which enclosed the glory of his family. He indulged the feelings of a parent and of a Christian. He sorrowed, but his sorrow was relieved and cheered by hope. If a pagan philosopher,[1] during one of those intervals in which truth shed a brighter ray on his expanding mind, could introduce the elder Cato hailing the glorious day when he should depart from this scene of tumult and confusion and repair to

---

1   Cicero *De Senectute*, cap. xxiii

the divine concourse and assembly of souls; when, in particular, he should go to his beloved son, whom he had prematurely consigned to the ravages of mortality but whose parting spirit, in its flight to the happy regions, had looked back upon him with the tender intimation that their real union was unbroken; while he could, in the meantime, console himself with the reflection that their separation would not be long—with how much greater, because more enlightened, confidence, might this Christian father cherish similar anticipations and, amid his bereavement, triumph in the thought that heaven was become the richer for his loss and the more his proper home than it had been before!

Funeral sermons were preached in each of the Methodist chapels at Liverpool and in all the other stations which Mr. Stoner had occupied. Vast crowds attended in every place to express their respect for his memory and to receive another testimony of the hallowing direction which religion gives to life, and of the powerful support which it ministers in death.

Judging according to the measurements and calculations of days and years, Mr. Stoner's life was short; but in assiduous labour and beneficial effects, it was long. He performed much in the limited space which was allotted to him. From the time of his early conversion he crowded the different periods of his earthly existence with exercises corresponding to their requirements. After commencing his pulpit efforts, he preached four thousand and forty-three times; not to mention an almost countless number of exhortations, advices, and prayers. *How* he passed through these duties the preceding pages testify. It may be safely said of him that, like Enoch, the youthful patriarch of the antediluvian world, "he, being made perfect in a short time, fulfilled a long time;" and that many Christian ministers, whose life has been lengthened to old age, have, in vigorous endeavour and extensive success, accomplished far less than he.

To himself the change is unutterably happy. While sorrowing recollection lingers over the circumstances of his departure, how obvious and moving is the Psalmist's sentiment: "As for man, his days are as grass: as a flower of the field, so he flourished. For the wind passeth over it, and it is gone!" But with this sentiment let the "everlasting mercy of the Lord" be associated. "Life and incorruption are brought to light." The frail texture which is dishevelled in the blast and withered in the dust shall spring afresh; and meanwhile, the fair flower of spiritual excellency shall bloom in a milder and better clime, spread its leaves to the uncreated sun of light and glory, and flourish in the beauties of immortality. "The hope of the ungodly," says an apocryphal writer, "is like thistledown that is blown away with the wind; like a thin froth that is driven away with the storm; like as the smoke which is dispersed here and there with a tempest and passeth away as the remembrance of a guest that tarrieth but a day. But the righteous live for evermore; their reward also is with the Lord, and the care of them is with the Most High."[1]

---

1 Wisdom of Solomon, v. 14, 15.

10
Character Summary

A description of his character, containing a brief view of his qualities

I. Of his intellectual ability: strength, soundness, and activity of mind, unyielding decision, and peculiar facility of adapting his instructions to the circumstances and capacities of different persons.

II. Of his religious attainments: enlightened assurance, humility, prayerfulness, habitual faith, love, diligent attention to the performance of every practical duty, and large enjoyment of spiritual happiness, notwithstanding his constitutional tendency to dejection.

III. Of his more observable habits external appearance: seeming repulsiveness of manner, taciturnity in company, free and unrestrained affability among his confidential friends, and remarkable exactness in all his plans and proceedings.

IV. Of his pulpit qualifications: choice of subjects, careful preparation of his sermons, style, mode of delivery, incessant solicitude to do good, and powerful effect of his ministry. Conclusion.

Here the compilers might finish their task and retire from a field which they trust has yielded both pleasant and profitable fruit. The character of this exemplary man is largely traced in the preceding pages, where its virtues are disclosed under the varying yet consistent aspects which they assumed in the successive periods of his life, and are illustrated by authentic and satisfactory documents. Several important particulars, however, have been unavoidably omitted; and it now appears not improper, in compliance with the ordinary usages of biography, to present at one view a combined delineation of the whole.

To attempt this may expose the writers to the suspicion of indulging in vain panegyric. Imaginary excellencies, it may be said, are easily portrayed under the guise of a real name; and that is sometimes attributed to man which is due only to God. Against these evils they would religiously guard. They wish to attire the subject of their affectionate recollections in no virtue which he did not possess, and to ascribe nothing to him beyond a diligent and faithful use of the supplies which he received from a higher source. God is the "Author of all good in man," and it is his glory which appears in examples of unaffected piety. He is the rich assemblage of perfection; and if it is right to celebrate every lovely impress which he has stamped on *material* creation—on the heavens which shine in his splendour and the earth which blooms with his beauty—it is certainly right to exhibit the brighter and holier discoveries of himself which are found in the *spiritual* excellencies of his devoted servants. These contribute to the advancement of his praise, and they may undoubtedly be described without robbing him of the "honour due unto his name" or idolatrously exalting the creature.

One observation the reader himself will have made: that all the gifts which adorn Mr. Stoner's character and entitle him to grateful remembrance flowed from his religion. But for this, he might have passed through life unnoted and unknown. Religion called him forth, roused his latent powers, and gave him that beneficial influence which he exercised over the minds of others. It is this which recommends him to special regard. The soul of man, breathed originally into his earthly frame by God himself and destined to an interminable duration, possesses astonishing energies; and these, as the records of history largely declare, may be excited by inferior motives; but it is only when controlled and governed by religion that they acquire the best and truest distinction. God has "poured the seed of immortality into the human breast," and nothing can be more delightful than to behold that seed cultivated by his own hand and producing a harvest to his praise.

In surveying the INTELLECTUAL ABILITY of Mr. Stoner, the first quality which invites our attention is *strength of mind*. Genius, perhaps, he had not—whether that term be employed, in its higher sense, to express the faculty which enlarges the ordinary bounds of knowledge and produces the treasure of original thought—or confined to its inferior but significant application as designating that vigour of imagination which arrays known truth in new imagery and felicitous combinations. Some tokens, indeed, of these properties occasionally appeared in his productions; but they were not sufficient to constitute character. His mental powers were plain, masculine, and searching. Nothing which came within the ordinary range of human meditation created him much difficulty. He could readily apprehend any subject that was presented to his notice and investigate it with ease and pleasure.

Associated with this was an eminent degree of what has been denominated *soundness of mind*. In the history of the human understanding, not a few instances occur of considerable intellectual talent debased by irregularity and eccentricity. Perhaps the mind, not satisfied with its just pretensions, has aspired to the envied endowments of genius and, failing in its efforts, has at length sought repose in the imitation of its fancied peculiarities. Unable to attain the *thing*, it has satisfied itself and amused others by seizing the *defect* with which it may incidentally be shaded. Nothing of this kind appeared in Mr. Stoner. His judgment was remarkably cautious, exact, and discriminating. Everyone would have pronounced him to be a man of good sense. He confined himself within the limits of his own powers, and nicely examined every point which fell under his notice. This quality particularly discovered itself when he selected materials from the productions of others. His sermons, often preached in different places, on the "Witness of the Spirit" and "Christian Perfection" are examples. They are drawn almost entirely from different parts of the works of the Rev. Messrs. Wesley and Fletcher, but are composed with excellent judgment. He once recommended to a friend the compilation of a body of theology extracted from the works and expressed in the words of Messrs. Wesley and Fletcher. For such a performance he was himself admirably qualified by his sagacity, care, and patience. It may be observed in passing that to the student of theology the quality just noted is truly inestimable. He has no new truth to discover. All his stores are contained in the sacred volume.

His task, therefore, is neither to soar into the regions of fancy, nor to oppress his memory with the unexamined productions of men, and then dignify the mingled mass with the title of theology; but to "compare spiritual things with spiritual," to trace the system of eternal truth as it is gradually unfolded in the Holy Oracles, and to avail himself of every help by patient meditation, by discriminating skill, and by what is equally a proof of sound intellect and correct feeling—prayerful dependence on the "Father of lights."

But the properties already mentioned may exist unemployed. Many a person possessing sound and vigorous powers accomplishes nothing because he attempts nothing. Mr. Stoner, however, was distinguished by *activity of mind*. In his select and various reading, in the diligence which he bestowed on the composition of every sermon, and in his perpetual habit of observant thought, he afforded sufficient evidence that, in the pursuit of its proper objects, his intellectual faculty was unweariable. The different manuscripts which he has left are truly surprising. They contain notices of almost everything that transpired in his official proceedings, collections of facts, remarks, etc., and are kept with such order and regularity as could have been secured only by a mind that had resolutely shaken off the shackles of indolence. His ceaseless activity of observation when in the company of others was not always apparent. He assumed no sagacity of aspect. Scarcely anything moved his quiet and settled features. To a superficial spectator he would sometimes seem lost in abstraction and almost totally inattentive to what transpired around him, while at the same moment he was making useful reflections on everything, however minute. It was partly in consequence of this that he possessed so accurate a knowledge of the human character in its multiplied varieties, and was so well skilled in touching the secret springs of motive and action.

His *decision of mind* was very observable. In his self-examinations, indeed, he often complains of instability; but this his most intimate friends could not discover. His firmness was unshaken. Wherever he saw the path of duty opening before him, he was determined to pursue it at the risk of all consequences. "His stern integrity," says Dr. McAllum, "was altogether uncompromising. He suffered no worldly considerations to swerve him from the path of uprightness." It deserves remark that this decision was not sustained by mere strength of nerve, nor was it the forced and feverish decision of occasional persuasion and excitement; it was the decision of *principle*—a decision which, had he lived in the perilous times of the church, would have assisted him to make the sacrifices of a confessor or suffer the death of a martyr. He had examined his ground; he had fixed his choice; and he was resolved to prosecute his course through "evil report and good report." Sometimes his firmness was suspected to partake, in a small degree, of obstinacy and stupidity; yet this suspicion was grounded chiefly on appearance. When just occasion required, he was generally very yielding; and if at some times he was not sufficiently attentive to the courtesies of social life, it can only be regretted that his inflexible determination should have partaken of any such alloy. Where truth and duty interpose their claims, no man ought to yield in the smallest particular to counter-solicitation; but in things perfectly indifferent, and in the expression even of firm sentiment, much is unquestionably due to the society in which we live and of which we form a part.

Another excellency of Mr. Stoner's intellectual character disclosed itself in the *facility* which he possessed *of adapting his communications to the circumstances and capacities of the different persons* with whom he had intercourse. This often appeared in his epistolary correspondence, but was chiefly observable in his public teaching. He studied character and capacity; he sought out acceptable and suitable expressions; he became "all things to all men, that he might by all means save some." It was extraordinary to those who knew him only superficially that one of his reserved and retiring temper could so easily seize the current of thought which was passing in another's mind, make "manifest the secrets of his heart," and present instruction in that form which at once shed light into the understanding and opened all the sources of serious feeling. This perhaps was one cause of the mighty influence which his modest and unpretending mind had over others. The most ignorant could easily receive instruction from Mr. Stoner, while the most skilful were delighted and profited by his luminous statements and comprehensive wisdom. Upon the whole, it may be pronounced that the powers of his mind were solid and useful rather than brilliant; and that they were conscientiously and diligently employed in their proper exercises; while their improvement and application ought to teach others that the proper method of honouring the great Author of all mind in his gifts is not to grasp at intellectual powers which they have not, but diligently and faithfully to use what they have.

THE RELIGIOUS ATTAINMENTS of Mr. Stoner were of no ordinary cast. "His piety," says Mr. Entwisle, "was deep and genuine. He was entirely devoted to God." "Everything," observes Dr. McAllum, "bespoke him a whole-length Christian—one who desired that his entire conversation and life and temper should be spiritual and unearthly." It will not be unprofitable to take a separate view of some of the more prominent features by which his religious character was distinguished.

One of these was his *enlightened assurance.* He regarded Christianity not as a system of conjecture, doubt, and uncertainty, but of bright and cheering testimony, conveying to the soul of the believer a satisfying evidence of the reconciling mercy and perpetual favour of God. He could not, therefore, be content without an humble assurance of his acceptance in Christ, and of the growing renovation of his nature. From the period of his sound and scriptural conversion, he endeavoured to lay his foundation in light and to seek light in its purer effusions and more powerful efficacy. Nor was he disappointed. He proved the truth of that saying, "Blessed is the people that know the joyful sound: they shall walk, O Lord, in the light of thy countenance."

The doctrine of assurance has been said to engender pride. This groundless allegation will not be advanced in the case of Mr. Stoner. In him scriptural assurance was associated with the deepest self-abasement. He was eminently "clothed with *humility.*" The records which he has left of his religious experience sufficiently testify how vigilant he was to guard against the first approaches of pride, and how accustomed to sink into the depths of his own nothingness, and rise to the most devout and reverential apprehensions of the divine purity and majesty. Sometimes his humility seems to have been employed by his spiritual adversaries to his discouragement, and it certainly concealed from others many of the attainments which he possessed. "He was little," remarks Dr. McAllum, "very little in his own eyes. Self-abasement was in him habitual, and from a certain constitutional sadness would have sunk him into despair but for the eminent measure of grace with which he was blessed." His humility discovered itself to others in a very observable manner amid the popularity which he possessed as a preacher. Of that popularity he seemed quite unconscious. So fully was his soul engrossed by other things that he had no attention to bestow on public commendation. "His eye," observes Mr. Entwisle, "was single. When with me at Bradford he was the most popular of all I have known in his regular Circuit work; but I could never perceive that his popularity gratified him. I have frequently known him reprove people for leaving their own places of worship to hear him. He felt his responsibility to God; he longed for the salvation of souls; he 'travailed in birth until Christ was formed in them;' and was unconcerned about the praises and censures of men. In all my intercourse with him for two years—and he resided next door to me—I never heard a word or observed a look, attitude, or any other circumstance which indicated aught tending to vanity, self-seeking, or the desire of honour that cometh from men. He fixed the standard of Christianity and of the Christian ministry very high and seemed to himself to come so far short of what he should be and enjoy as a Christian and a preacher that he was often discouraged. Not unfrequently, when he was applauded by others, and justly so, he was employed in humbling himself before God. He thought very meanly of his best performances." Similar observations were made on his temper and conduct in all his other stations. He ever loved to hide himself in the dust before God and to shun the commendation of man. What is said of an illustrious senator of antiquity may be justly applied to him, "He rather wished to *be*, than to *appear*, good."[1]

Humility is the parent of *prayer*, and of Mr. Stoner's unceasing attention to this duty no person who has read the preceding pages of these memoirs can be ignorant. Prayer mingled itself with all his

---

1   "Esse, quam videri, bonus malebat." Sallust, *Bellum Catilinae* (54.6),

studies and exertions. In private, in his family, in public, he was continually a man of prayer. If all the time could be calculated which he spent in the direct performance of this duty it would amount to no inconsiderable portion of his life. He was unwearied in recommending prayer to others as one who knew from experience its mighty efficacy. "Prayer," says Tertullian, "conquers the Unconquerable and binds the Omnipotent; this violence is pleasing to God." It is the means by which he has appointed that his people shall prevail with him. So Mr. Stoner often found it. Of his attention to public prayer-meetings much has already been said. "Wherever it was practicable," says the Rev. William Clegg, "it was usual with him to hold prayer-meetings after his sermons; and on these occasions he would pray twice, or thrice, or oftener, as if he was in an agony that God would pour out an overwhelming influence upon the people, in order that the ignorant might be convinced, the guilty pardoned, and believers established in faith and love. I was with him once or twice at meetings of this kind; and if the powers of recollection continue, never shall I forget what I felt and heard and saw."

"He might indeed be said," remarks Mr. Entwisle, "to give himself unto prayer. He prayed and wrestled earnestly with God for his presence and unction and for a blessing on his labours. To this ought to be attributed the extraordinary power and unction and success of his public ministrations." His last breath was prayer.

Faith also was a very prominent part of his religious character—not merely in its occasional acts, but in its habitual and constant exercise. He largely possessed the "*spirit* of faith." Hence he continually sought to know God's will, gave explicit credit to every declaration of his Word, and reposed the full confidence of his soul on the merits of his crucified Redeemer. With the holy apostle he could say, "I am crucified with Christ: nevertheless I live; yet not I, but Christ liveth in me; and the life which I now live in the flesh I live by the faith of the Son of God, who loved me, and gave himself for me." His faith constantly acknowledged the promises which speak of an abundant communication of divine influence. Of this he had enlarged and elevated views and diligently sought it for himself and for others. His firm faith in the power and agency of the Holy Spirit manifested itself in all his public work and gave an uncommon force to his pulpit ministrations. He preached in faith, and very often "according to his faith it was done unto him."

For every exercise of *love*, that crowning virtue of the Christian character, he was truly exemplary. His love to God was a feeling of supreme veneration, of exclusive preference, of filial attachment, of calm delight, and unreserved submissions. The habitual language of his soul was, "Whom have I in heaven hut thee? and there is none upon earth that I desire beside thee." His love to his fellow Christians was a love of sincere fraternal affection. He regarded them as brethren in Christ and entered with peculiar interest into all the pleasures of communion with them. To himself no ordinances were more desirable or profitable than meetings of spiritually-minded believers for the purposes of prayer and Christian fellowship. At such meetings, whether he declared what God had "done for his own soul," or listened to the simple and impressive statements of others, he felt himself more than usually at home. His love to sinners was an ardent and unceasing compassion. Painfully aware of the miseries, present and future, to which they are exposed, he thought no sacrifice too severe, no effort too great, no prayer too fervent, if he might only be the honoured instrument of saving one soul from death. This sentiment attended him through life and, as has been related already, breathed itself forth in the last words which fell from his dying lips.

His *diligent attention to the performance of every practical duty* ought not to escape remark. In all things that related to personal holiness, of life as well as of heart, he was an instructive pattern. "He thought of no abatement," says Dr. McAllum, "from the sterling weights of the sanctuary; and though he was far enough from hoping for justification by the works of the law, he never doubted that we are called to perfect holiness in the fear of the Lord, and that grace is all-sufficient to that end." In the discharge of relative duty, as a son, a brother, a husband, a father, a master, he was eminently amiable and faithful, especially caring for the spiritual interests of all with whom he was connected. Dr. McAllum particularly mentions the care which he bestowed on the religious education of his children. He was also uncommonly assiduous in performing the pastoral duties of his office, in spite of the timidity and reluctance of his nature. To the sick and poor he was uncommonly attentive. "Indeed," to adopt the testimony of Mr. Entwisle, "in every part of his work as a Methodist preacher he was habitually diligent. He practically attended to that rule of a helper, 'Never be unemployed. Never be triflingly employed. Never while away time.' His application to reading, study, and prayer in reference to his great work was prodigious. He seemed to grudge every moment that was not employed to some good purpose. A very large proportion of his time was spent in his study; and yet to visit a sick person, or to assist his colleague in any way whatever, he would at any time quit his beloved retirement with cheerful promptitude. He attended to every part of Methodism. He observed every movement and was always ready to check evil and promote good. In the year 1821, I was about three months from home, in Ireland, etc. We had been blessed with a large increase to our societies and the young converts wanted nursing. He wrote to me frequently and mentioned everything of importance that occurred, whether pleasing or painful; so that I was nearly as well acquainted with the state of the societies as if I had been with him. In a word, he uniformly gave himself to the work of a Methodist preacher, both in public and private." It ought to be added that in the exercise of pecuniary charity he was remarkably liberal. Limited as his income was, he invariably appropriated a certain portion of it to charitable uses and would not, on any consideration, employ that sum for other purposes. Dr. McAllum, who was intimately acquainted with his proceedings, emphatically pronounces him "a truly generous man;" and adds, "A more cheerful giver I never knew."

In closing the review of his religious character it may be confidently affirmed that he enjoyed a large portion of *spiritual happiness.* He had indeed a constitutional bias to dejection, and he suffered much from the various trials by which the Christian is assailed in his earthly warfare. Yet his was a religion of heartfelt peace. "Light is sown for the righteous," and from that seed he was enabled to reap a blessed harvest. Amid all the changes of life and variations of feeling, he generally retained a clear evidence of his heavenly Father's love; he had free access to the throne of grace; and he could rejoice in hope of future glory. There were seasons when his head was more plentifully anointed with the "oil of gladness" and when his cup of blessing ran over. At such times he felt the well of living water which had been opened in his soul springing up with more copious and refreshing supplies "into everlasting life;" he tasted of a secret joy, with which the stranger-world does not intermeddle—a joy unspeakably "superior to the wanton levity of mirth, calm, silent, and solemn; the sublime fruition of truth and virtue." In true spiritual repose, and in the enjoyment of that high felicity for which man was born, one hour of Mr. Stoner's happy intercourse with God would outweigh an age spent in the pleasures of sin. To that comprehensive saying he could without hesitation affix the seal of his personal experience, "The ways of wisdom are ways of pleasantness, and *all* her paths are peace."

To mention a few of his more observable HABITS may assist in conveying a full view of the man. He was tall in his person and extremely plain in his dress. His countenance was expressive of a serious, devout, and sensible mind; but his general *appearance* was rather uninviting. There were few persons, who had heard of his excellencies only by report, that did not feel a slight disappointment when they first saw him. He resembled "a rich stone set in lead," and it was necessary to have some acquaintance with him in order to know his real value.

His *seeming repulsiveness of manner*, especially to entire strangers, was often remarked. "The first thought which occurred to anyone," says Dr. McAllum, "on being introduced to him was, 'He is a man of an austere look, and his words are abrupt to the verge of harshness.'" This, however, could only be a *first* impression. "It soon appeared to those," adds the Doctor, "who were privileged with his friendship, that this austerity of look and manner arose from nothing haughty or repulsive, selfish or unkind, in his temper; but was produced by a certain diffidence and distrust of himself which made him shrink from society as anxiously as many seek it. There was a constitutional reserve about him, only to be broken through by long acquaintance and much perseverance; and when at length any one succeeded in making him at ease, his spirit was felt to be as kindly and agreeable as it was devoted and alive to God." From his private papers it sufficiently appears how much the infirmity above mentioned distressed his own mind and how earnestly he desired to be delivered from it. It is probable that his struggle against it terminated only with his life.

To the above must be added his remarkable *taciturnity* in mixed company. It seemed almost impossible to draw him out in conversation. This defect also, which flowed from the same cause with the former one, he sincerely lamented; but he could not entirely subdue it. "Often," said he, "have I paced my room for hours wondering how the providence of God had ever brought me into so public a station, for which my temper is so little fit; for if my life depended upon it, I could not feel at ease with more than a few."

"He sat in bondage and pain," observes Mr. Entwisle, "especially if the company was large and respectable. Some persons were grieved and almost offended at his reserve. So they termed it. But I can say, without hesitation, that on such occasions he generally felt much more pain than others."

In the society of a few confidential friends, however, he was eminent for a *free and unrestrained affability*. His company at such times was extremely agreeable. There was an uncommon blandness in his countenance, tone, and manner. He abounded in anecdote, and sometimes indulged in a considerable degree of innocent pleasantry and humour. His taciturn temper seemed entirely to forsake him, and he laid open with the most unsuspecting confidence the secret recesses of his heart. His familiar associates were, therefore, very warmly attached to him, and seemed to retain no impression of that bashful and retiring demeanour which others could not but observe.

The *exactness* which he observed in all his plans and proceedings may not improperly be mentioned here. He possessed, in an extraordinary degree, the love of order. A slave to regularity indeed he was not, but he successfully pressed it into his service. All things were judiciously, but not servilely, arranged; and so diligently had he attended to accuracy that it appeared even in the most minute particulars. In all his manuscripts, which were, of course, prepared only for his own use, there are very few erasures; in the short-hand with which they are largely interspersed there is scarcely a single instance of deviation from the system which he had adopted, or of mistake; and, so far as the writers have examined them, not one example of false spelling. These things, trivial as they may be deemed by some, show his habitual exactness, and afford an instance of the possibility of being regular without stiffness, and correct without servility.

Of his PULPIT QUALIFICATIONS it remains that a short account be given; and after the observations which have been advanced in different parts of the memoirs, a short account will suffice.

In the *choice of his subjects* he was very conscientious and careful. His inquiry was not, What subject will afford the amplest scope for theological research, bring forth to greatest advantage the materials of my reading, or give the richest variety to my public ministrations? but, What subject is likely, by the blessing of God, to be most useful? To this point he confined his attention. The greater part of his sermons were of an awakening character, for that was his special talent; several were employed in recommending the privileges of the Christian, and particularly in enforcing entire holiness; and not a few were devoted to the cheering and encouraging topics of evangelical consolation. All the texts from which he ever preached are recorded in the books which he kept for the purpose, and they furnish an admirable collection of appropriate passages for the pulpit.

On the *preparation* of his sermons he bestowed much care. Latterly, indeed, he seems on some occasions to have penned only a few short notes; but his general practice was to write the whole, or nearly the whole, at full length. To this practice, not commendable certainly in every case, he had been partly led in early life by a fear that he should not have a sufficient degree of self-possession in the pulpit to command suitable language; and he had by degrees formed it into an easy habit. Fluent indeed as he was, when he had made his usual preparation, it may be questioned whether he would have excelled as a purely extemporary speaker. On the missionary platform, where extemporary addresses are almost indispensable, he was not at all extraordinary; though no man could feel more deeply concerned than he for the conversion of the heathen world. It ought to be remarked that his sermons suffered nothing, in point of effect, from the exact manner in which they were prepared. They had all the life and vigour of earnest and unpremeditated address. It is only necessary further to say that every sermon was skilfully arranged—crowded, sometimes perhaps to excess, with useful matter—and adapted, in all its parts, to furnish instruction and produce conviction.

"The *style* of his discourses," observes Dr. McAllum, "was remarkably simple, pure, and forceful. He was never coarse or vulgar, but he was easy to be understood. His words were all of them sought out and selected on the principle of being the most familiar in which his ideas could be conveyed. For the same reason, his sentences were short and clear in their structure; neither loaded nor involved, but perspicuous and intelligible. He no more thought that what was perspicuous must be superficial than that what was perplexed must be profound. His style was not meagre but enriched with the purest and most classical terms which the example of the best writers has sanctioned among us. His were right words and full of force; they had all the energy of compactness, of an equal structure that labours under weakness in no one part; they were condensed to energy and precision. He never mistook size for vigour nor sacrificed specific gravity to bulk."

To the remarks of this excellent judge of composition it may be subjoined that Mr. Stoner by no means affected the laconic style. In the opinion of some, his diction was copious to an extreme. Yet Mr. Turton has correctly observed that scarcely anything was really "redundant." "Expressions nearly the same in sense were employed in a very skilful manner, each succeeding one adding something to the beauty and force of what had gone before"—an observation this which the writers have repeatedly had occasion to make in the examination of Mr. Stoner's manuscripts.

His *mode of delivery* was quite consistent with his general habits. He was deeply serious. He had little or no action except a slight inclination of the body forward in the more animated parts of his discourse. At all times he was earnest but never vociferous. It has already been mentioned more than once that his utterance was rapid—yet not unpleasantly so. "Though rapid," observes Dr. McAllum, "it was perfectly clear; every word fell full and distinct upon the ear; and its very rapidity fixed attention and by that means gave the more effect to his discourse." In securing attention indeed he was remarkable. Some parts of his delivery, if judged by the rules of rhetoricians, would be pronounced defective; but its defects were forgotten amid the deep and fixed regard which he excited. "I have seen numbers of his hearers," says Mr. Turton, "rise almost involuntarily soon after he has begun his sermon and remain on their feet to the end, so powerfully attracted by what they were hearing that they seemed unable to sit down."

No person could attend his ministry, either regularly or occasionally, without being struck with his *incessant solicitude to do good*. Every other consideration was swallowed up in this. "His prayer," remarks Dr. McAllum, "was, 'Never may I preach one useless sermon;' and the sermon under which believers were not strengthened or sinners awakened was, he thought, a useless one. With all his heart, soul, mind, and strength he aimed at usefulness, and especially at awakening, quickening, and informing the conscience; and that not merely in the application of his discourses, but throughout the whole of them, from the commencement to the close. The sword he wielded was of keen edge from the hilt to the point. There was a certain peculiarity in his sermons. At the close of a paragraph he would utter a petition suited to the tenor of it. After describing holiness in any of its beauties, for instance, he would exclaim, 'The Lord sanctify each of us!' Or, after describing the displeasure of God in any one of its frowns, he would pray, 'The Lord save us from the wrath to come!' Knowing the terrors of the Lord, he persuaded men, and preached as one who had death and judgment, heaven and hell, full in his eye—as if this was the latest and the only opportunity of winning trophies to redeeming power and of plucking brands from the burning. The thought of self entirely disappeared in the great business of delivering his message and gaining attention to it. In his pulpit appearances there was no one thing which could be mistaken as indicating a theorist or a feeling of the honour that cometh from man. On the contrary, he laboured instantly like one overwhelmed with the conviction that souls were *now* perishing and that this was the only day of salvation. The hearer was never allowed to think of the preacher or of the composition; all his thoughts and concerns were forced in upon himself; and he went away saying, not, 'What a great sermon have I heard' but, 'God be merciful to me a sinner!' Appeal following appeal lightened upon the conscience, revealing at once the darkness and the light; the 'strong man' trembled to be dispossessed of his goods; but bolt succeeded bolt till the building was shaken from the foundation to the corner-stone. To appearance, he put all his strength into every sermon. Spiritual profit, the utmost profit, and present profit was the thing aimed at, and by the blessing of God secured to most, by his sermons. The ruling passion, the ceaseless spring, the vehement thirst of his soul was to do good. The zeal of the Lord ate him up. It was a fire in his bones. It was a torrent on his lips, for the mouth of the just is a well-spring of life. When there was a prospect of doing good, he conferred not with flesh and blood; for he loved the Lord with all his strength; and hence, after preaching thrice and travelling in the country, he has often spent some hours in a prayer-meeting, frequently engaging in prayer, in exhortation, and in praise. His zeal was not mere excitement—it was a stream whose strength is not in its current merely but in its volume of water."

"In the sermons I heard from him," remarks Mr. Clegg, "there was no appearance of design to preach in a learned, eloquent, or eccentric manner, but to pour out as rapidly as possible a torrent of divine truth into the heads and hearts of his hearers, and then to direct it in various streams to their different characters and consciences, commonly concluding his numerous applications with a fervent prayer to God that he would make his word effectual to the salvation of the people. In short, whether he preached in aid of missions, chapels, or Sunday schools, he seemed to aim directly at the great object of his ministry—to turn his hearers, at the time he addressed them, from darkness to light, and from the power of Satan unto God. His preaching had not only a tendency to do good to sinners and private Christians but also to ministers of the gospel. It was scarcely possible for them to hear him without feeling the vast importance of a faithful ministry and forming purposes to be more urgent in the great work of winning souls."

That the *effect* of such a ministry should be unusually *powerful* is not surprising. Of Mr. Stoner it may emphatically be said that "by manifestation of the truth he commended himself to every man's conscience in the sight of God." He was an honoured instrument in the edifying of Christian believers and the conversion of hundreds, perhaps thousands, of sinners. "Few men," observes Mr. Entwisle, "since the commencement of the work of God under the name of Methodism, have been so successful in the conversion of sinners from the error of their ways. I speak from my own knowledge on this subject. During the two years we were together at Bradford, a great number, I will not presume to say how many, were convinced of sin under his preaching. The hand of God was eminently with him."

"When I went to the Keighley Circuit in 1822," says Mr. Clegg, "I soon found that I was surrounded by persons who were attributing their spiritual conversion and happiness to his instrumentality, and that he was very popular through all the country around. But this popularity was of the very best kind. God had been pleased to honour him with such amazing usefulness at Bradford and other places in the neighbourhood that the people crowded in immense numbers to hear him. They esteemed him as an extraordinary messenger from God. They went to hear him with religious feeling and ardent expectation, hoping and praying that God would there and then pour out his Holy Spirit in a rich effusion and greatly revive and extend his work; and so far as I had the opportunity of observing, they were not disappointed."

And here the writers conclude their record of the life and ministry of DAVID STONER. Short as was his temporal day, they doubt not that he will occupy an honourable place among them who having "turned many to righteousness" shall "shine as the stars for ever and ever." He has "died in the Lord." He "rests from his labours and his works do follow him." It is a cheering reflection that God, who gave him for a season to that section of his church to which he was united, can easily raise up others such as he. The "residue of the Spirit is with him." Let prayer be offered that he would furnish a succession of faithful and zealous ministers whose trumpet—whether they publish an alarm to sinners—summon the "sacramental host of his elect" to warfare—or invite them to share in the festivities of his love—shall give no "uncertain sound;" but who shall continue from time to time to utter the powerful and distinct notes of evangelical truth and mercy until another trumpet shall pour its awful sounds through the immensity of space, rouse the dead to life, and usher in the "great and terrible day of the Lord."

That day approaches. The providential government of God moves on amid the fluctuations and changes of time; it is guided, beyond the conception and control of man, by his own wisdom, power, and love; and it will, ere long, be consummated to the "praise of his glory." All mysteries shall then be unravelled. The righteous destiny of every rational and accountable intelligence shall be fixed, and nothing shall continue but solemn, eternal, unchanging reality.

"It remains," to adopt the sentiments of the most eloquent of the Latin Fathers,[1] "that we exhort all to embrace wisdom and true religion, the powerful obligations of which require us to despise earthly objects, to renounce the errors by which we were formerly enslaved when we served and coveted perishable enjoyments, and to direct our full attention to the everlasting rewards of the heavenly treasure. To obtain these, the enticing pleasures of this present life, which captivate the minds of men by their pernicious sweetness, must immediately be relinquished. How highly ought we to estimate the felicity of retiring from the disorders of the earth and repairing to him who is our most equitable Judge and most indulgent Parent, who bestows rest for labour, life for death, for darkness light, and for advantages which are earthly and fleeting such as are eternal and heavenly! With these the sufferings and distresses which we endure in this world, while we perform the works of righteousness, can by no means be equalled or compared.

It is, then, the indispensable duty of all to give diligence that their feet may be guided without delay into the right path, and that having commenced and perfected their virtues and patiently borne the toils of this life, they may be accounted worthy to enjoy the consolation of God. For our Father and Lord, who founded and established the heaven, who lighted up the sun and stars, who, poising the earth by its own magnitude fortified it with mountains, encompassed it by

---

1 Lactantius, ivth Inst., lib. vii. 27.

the ocean, and intersected it with rivers, who, in a word, moulded and completed out of nothing all that exists in this fabric of the universe—He, surveying the errors of men, has sent a Leader to open to us the way of righteousness. Him let us all follow; him let us hear; to him let us render devoted obedience; for he only, as Lucretius says,

> With truth-instilling words the soul of man
> Has purged, the bounds of wishing and of fear
> Pointed precise, and show'd—
> The good supreme we all would fain possess
> Has oped its essence, has the path disclosed,
> Narrow but straight, that leads us where it dwells.[2]

Let us forsake the path of fraud and perdition in which death lies concealed under the blandishments of pleasure. Let every one who, while his years are verging to age, sees that day approaching in which he must remove from this life, consider how pure he may depart and how spotless he may approach his Judge. Let him not imitate those who, in the blindness of their minds, even when the strength of their body is already failing and they are warned by this of the pressing approach of their last extremity, are devoting themselves more greedily and ardently than ever to the gratification of their immoderate desires. From this gulf let everyone escape while he may, while the opportunity is afforded, and let him turn to God with his whole heart; that he may securely await that day in which the Governor and Lord of the world shall pronounce judgment on every man's deeds and thoughts. Let him not only disregard, but flee, the earthly things which others eagerly desire, and judge that his soul is of far greater value than those fallacious advantages. The possession of them is uncertain and frail. They are flitting daily, and depart much more swiftly than they came; and yet if we were allowed to enjoy them even to the last, we must certainly then resign them to others. He will be found truly rich before God who maintains temperance, mercy, patience, charity, faith. This is our heritage, which cannot be torn from one or transferred to another. And who is he that would secure these benefits for himself? Let them who hunger come, that,

---

2   Lucretius, lib. vi. 22-27. Good's translation slightly altered.

filled with celestial food, they may satisfy their continual famine. Let them who thirst come, that they may draw the water of salvation in richest draughts from a perennial and celestial spring. Supplied with this food and drink of God, the blind shall see, the deaf shall hear, the dumb shall speak, the lame shall walk, the foolish shall be wise, the sick shall enjoy health, and the dead shall revive. Whoever, in the prosecution of heavenly virtue, shall have spurned the corruptions of earth, him the supreme and veracious Judge will raise to perpetual light and life. Let no person confide in riches, in civil dignities, or even in royal power: these things give not immortality. For every one who has abandoned the reason of man and, in pursuit of present objects has prostrated his nobler powers in the dust, shall be punished as a deserter from his Lord, his Commander, and his Father. Let us then vigorously aim at righteousness, which as an inseparable companion will alone conduct us to God; and while the vital spirit governs these limbs, let us war an unweariable warfare for God. Let us keep our stations and watches. Let us valiantly engage with the enemy, whom we know; that rising into victors and triumphing over the vanquished adversary, we may obtain from the Lord that recompense of virtue which he has promised.

Also from Kingsley Press:

An Ordered Life
An Autobiography by G. H. Lang

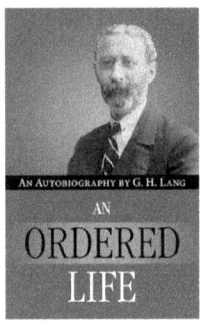

G. H. Lang was a remarkable Bible teacher, preacher and writer of a past generation who should not be forgotten by today's Christians. He inherited the spiritual "mantle" of such giants in the faith as George Müller, Anthony Norris Groves and other notable saints among the early Brethren movement. He traveled all over the world with no fixed means of support other than prayer and faith and no church or other organization to depend on. Like Mr. Müller before him, he told his needs to no one but God. Many times his faith was tried to the limit, as funds for the next part of his journey arrived only at the last minute and from unexpected sources.

This autobiography traces in precise detail the dealings of God with his soul, from the day of his conversion at the tender age of seven, through the twilight years when bodily infirmity restricted most of his former activities. You will be amazed, as you read these pages, to see how quickly and continually a soul can grow in grace and in the knowledge of spiritual things if they will wholly follow the Lord.

Horace Bushnell once wrote that every man's life is a plan of God, and that it's our duty as human beings to find and follow that plan. As Mr. Lang looks back over his long and varied life in the pages of this book, he frequently points out the many times God prepared him in the present for some future work or role. Spiritual life applications abound throughout the book, making it not just a life story but a spiritual training manual of sorts. Preachers will find sermon starters and illustrations in every chapter. Readers of all kinds will benefit from this close-up view of the dealings of God with the soul of one who made it his life's business to follow the Lamb wherever He should lead.

Buy online at our website: **www.KingsleyPress.com**
Also available as an eBook for Kindle, Nook and iBooks.

The Revival We Need

by Oswald J. Smith

When Oswald J. Smith wrote this book almost a hundred years ago he felt the most pressing need of the worldwide church was true revival—the kind birthed in desperate prayer and accompanied by deep conviction for sin, godly sorrow, and deep repentance, resulting in a living, victorious faith. If he were alive today he would surely conclude that the need has only become more acute with the passing years.

The author relates how there came a time in his own ministry when he became painfully aware that his efforts were not producing spiritual results. His intense study of the New Testament and past revivals only deepened this conviction. The Word of God, which had proved to be a hammer, a fire and a sword in the hands of apostles and revivalists of bygone days, was powerless in his hands. But as he prayed and sought God in dead earnest for the outpouring of the Holy Spirit, things began to change. Souls came under conviction, repented of their sins, and were lastingly changed.

The earlier chapters of the book contain Smith's heart-stirring messages on the need for authentic revival: how to prepare the way for the Spirit's moving, the tell-tale signs that the work is genuine, and the obstacles that can block up the channels of blessing. These chapters are laced with powerful quotations from revivalists and soul-winners of former times, such as David Brainerd, William Bramwell, John Wesley, Charles Finney, Evan Roberts and many others. The latter chapters detail Smith's own quest for the enduement of power, his soul-travail, and the spiritual fruit that followed.

In his foreword to this book, Jonathan Goforth writes, "Mr. Smith's book, *The Revival We Need*, for its size is the most powerful plea for revival I have ever read. He has truly been led by the Spirit of God in preparing it. To his emphasis for the need of a Holy Spirit revival I can give the heartiest amen. What I saw of revival in Korea and in China is in fullest accord with the revival called for in this book."

Buy online at our website: **www.KingsleyPress.com**
Also available as an eBook for Kindle, Nook and iBooks.

Lord, Teach Us to Pray
By Alexander Whyte

Dr. Alexander Whyte (1836-1921) was widely acknowledged to be the greatest Scottish preacher of his day. He was a mighty pulpit orator who thundered against sin, awakening the consciences of his hearers, and then gently leading them to the Savior. He was also a great teacher, who would teach a class of around 500 young men after Sunday night service, instructing them in the way of the Lord more perfectly.

In the later part of Dr. Whyte's ministry, one of his pet topics was prayer. Luke 11:1 was a favorite text and was often used in conjunction with another text as the basis for his sermons on this subject. The sermons printed here represent only a few of the many delivered. But each one is deeply instructive, powerful and convicting.

Nobody else could have preached these sermons; after much reading and re-reading of them that remains the most vivid impression. There can be few more strongly personal documents in the whole literature of the pulpit. . . . When all is said, there is something here that defies analysis—something titanic, something colossal, which makes ordinary preaching seem to lie a long way below such heights as gave the vision in these words, such forces as shaped their appeal. We are driven back on the mystery of a great soul, dealt with in God's secret ways and given more than the ordinary measure of endowment and grace. His hearers have often wondered at his sustained intensity; as Dr. Joseph Parker once wrote of him: "many would have announced the chaining of Satan for a thousand years with less expenditure of vital force" than Dr. Whyte gave to the mere announcing of a hymn. —*From the Preface*

Buy online at our website: **www.KingsleyPress.com**
Also available as an eBook for Kindle, Nook and iBooks.

The Way of the Cross
by J. Gregory Mantle

"DYING to self is the *one only way* to life in God," writes Dr. Mantle in this classic work on the cross. "The end of self is the one condition of the promised blessing, and he that is not willing to die to things sinful, *yea, and to things lawful,* if they come between the spirit and God, cannot enter that world of light and joy and peace, provided on this side of heaven's gates, where thoughts and wishes, words and works, delivered from the perverting power of self—revolve round Jesus Christ, as the planets revolve around the central sun....

"It is a law of dynamics that two objects cannot occupy the same space at the same time, and if we are ignorant of the crucifixion of the self-life as an experimental experience, we cannot be filled with the Holy Spirit. 'If thy heart,' says Arndt in his *True Christianity,* 'be full of the world, there will be no room for the Spirit of God to enter; for where the one is the other cannot be.' If, on the contrary, we have endorsed our Saviour's work as the destroyer of the works of the devil, and have claimed to the full the benefits of His death and risen life, what hinders the complete and abiding possession of our being by the Holy Spirit but our unbelief?"

Rev. J. Gregory Mantle (1853 - 1925) *had a wide and varied ministry in Great Britain, America, and around the world. For many years he was the well-loved Superintendent of the flourishing Central Hall in Deptford, England, as well as a popular speaker at Keswick and other large conventions for the deepening of spiritual life. He spent the last twelve years of his life in America, where he was associated with Dr. A. B. Simpson and the Christian and Missionary Alliance. He traveled extensively, holding missions and conventions all over the States. He was an avid supporter of foreign missions throughout his entire career. He also edited a missionary paper, and wrote several books.*

GIPSY SMITH
HIS LIFE AND WORK

This autobiography of Gipsy Smith (1860-1947) tells the fascinating story of how God's amazing grace reached down into the life of a poor, uneducated gipsy boy and sent him singing and preaching all over Britain and America until he became a household name in many parts and influenced the lives of millions for Christ. He was born and raised in a gipsy tent to parents who made a living selling baskets, tinware and clothes pegs. His father was in and out of jail for various offences, but was gloriously converted during an evangelistic meeting. His mother died when he was only five years old.

Converted at the age of sixteen, Gipsy taught himself to read and write and began to practice preaching. His beautiful singing voice earned him the nickname "the singing gipsy boy," as he sang hymns to the people he met. At age seventeen he became an evangelist with the Christian Mission (which became the Salvation Army) and began to attract large crowds. Leaving the Salvation Army in 1882, he became an itinerant evangelist working with a variety of organizations. It is said that he never had a meeting without conversions. He was a born orator. One of the Boston papers described him as "the greatest of his kind on earth, a spiritual phenomenon, an intellectual prodigy and a musical and oratorical paragon."

His autobiography is full of anedotes and stories from his preaching experiences in many different places. It's a book you won't want to put down until you're finished!

Buy online at our website: **www.KingsleyPress.com**
Also available as an eBook for Kindle, Nook and iBooks.

The Awakening
By Marie Monsen

REVIVAL! It was a long time coming. For twenty long years Marie Monsen prayed for revival in China. She had heard reports of how God's Spirit was being poured out in abundance in other countries, particularly in nearby Korea; so she began praying for funds to be able to travel there in order to bring back some of the glowing coals to her own mission field. But that was not God's way. The still, small voice of God seemed to whisper, "What is happening in Korea can happen in China if you will pay the price in prayer." Marie Monsen took up the challenge and gave her solemn promise: "Then I will pray until I receive."

The Awakening is Miss Monsen's own vivid account of the revival that came in answer to prayer. Leslie Lyall calls her the "pioneer" of the revival movement—the handmaiden upon whom the Spirit was first poured out. He writes: "Her surgical skill in exposing the sins hidden within the Church and lurking behind the smiling exterior of many a trusted Christian—even many a trusted Christian leader—and her quiet insistence on a clear-cut experience of the new birth set the pattern for others to follow."

The emphasis in these pages is on the place given to prayer both before and during the revival, as well as on the necessity of self-emptying, confession, and repentance in order to make way for the infilling of the Spirit.

One of the best ways to stir ourselves up to pray for revival in our own generation is to read the accounts of past awakenings, such as those found in the pages of this book. Surely God is looking for those in every generation who will solemnly take up the challenge and say, with Marie Monsen, "I will pray until I receive."

Buy online at our website: **www.KingsleyPress.com**
Also available as an eBook for Kindle, Nook and iBooks.

FIRSTFRUITS AND HARVEST
By G. H. Lang

Few writers have approached the subject of Biblical prophecy with more diligence and precise thinking than G. H. Lang. His purpose in studying and writing on the end-times and related themes was not to be controversial or sensational, but rather to encourage watchfulness and readiness. The serious reader will find much to challenge both mind and heart in these pages as the writer uses the prophetic Scriptures to give a strong call to holy and careful living.

The secret of G. H. Lang's power and persuasiveness as a writer must surely be attributed to his lifelong dedication to searching the Scriptures, not for the sake of aquiring more knowledge, but in order that he might know God more intimately and follow Him more closely. His great passion was that God's children everywhere would press beyond the shallow and superficial and into a deep understanding of the ways and workings of God. In this respect he was the true successor to such spiritual giants as George Müller, Hudson Taylor, Robert Cleaver Chapman and Anthony Norris Groves.

One of Mr. Lang's contemporaries, Douglas W. Brealey, wrote of him: "I think I may truthfully say that he was the most apostolic man I have ever met; perhaps for that very reason he was a very controversial figure; a correspondent suggested to me that he was the most controversial figure in Brethren circles since J. N. Darby; yet it would be true to say that he himself was not a controversialist. A very close student of the Word, and an independent thinker, he was not prepared to take traditional interpretations unless he were personally convinced that they were right.... To be in his presence was to realize that one was in the presence of a true saint of God whose holy life gave weight and authority to all he taught."

Buy online at our website: **www.KingsleyPress.com**
Also available as an eBook for Kindle, Nook and iBooks.

The Churches of God
by G. H. Lang

If you've ever wondered what the churches of the New Testament looked like—how they functioned, how they were governed, how they conducted their evangelistic and missionary enterprises, what ordinances they observed, what their liturgy consisted of, how decisions were made, how discipline was administered; if you've ever wondered how far modern churches have drifted from the New Testament pattern; if you've ever wondered what it would take for your church, and others like it, to return to the New Testament model, or if such a thing is even possible or desirable—then this book is for you!

G. H. Lang's ability to elucidate Biblical truth was never more evident than in this small treatise on the constitution, government, discipline and ministry of the church of God. His gifts as a diligent Bible student, expositor, and precise thinker, together with his many years of experience as an itinerant Bible teacher in many different countries and cultural settings, all combine to make this a go-to reference on many issues relating to the local church.

About the Author

G. H. Lang (1874-1958) was a gifted Bible teacher and prolific author who in his early life was associated with the "exclusive" branch of the Plymouth Brethren but later affiliated himself with the Open Brethren. He traveled widely as an itinerant Bible teacher, depending solely on God for his support. Although Mr. Lang himself was a prolific author, it was his belief that "no man should write a book until he is 40. He needs to prove his theories in practice before publishing." In his own case, all but nine of his many books were written after he was 50. Kingsley Press has recently re-published Lang's amazing autobiography, *An Ordered Life*. More information can be found on our web site: www.KingsleyPress.com.

A Present Help
By Marie Monsen

Does your faith in the God of the impossible need reviving? Do you think that stories of walls of fire and hosts of guardian angels protecting God's children are only for Bible times? Then you should read the amazing accounts in this book of how God and His unseen armies protected and guided Marie Monsen, a Norwegian missionary to China, as she traveled through bandit-ridden territory spreading the Gospel of Jesus Christ and standing on the promises of God. You will be amazed as she tells of an invading army of looters who ravaged a whole city, yet were not allowed to come near her mission compound because of angels standing sentry over it. Your heart will thrill as she tells of being held captive on a ship for twenty-three days by pirates whom God did not allow to harm her, but instead were compelled to listen to her message of a loving Savior who died for their sin. As you read the many stories in this small volume your faith will be strengthened by the realization that our God is a living God who can still bring protection and peace in the midst of the storms of distress, confusion and terror—a very present help in trouble.

Buy online at our website: **www.KingsleyPress.com**
Also available as an eBook for Kindle, Nook and iBooks.

ANTHONY NORRIS GROVES
SAINT AND PIONEER
by G. H. Lang

Although his name is little known in Christian cirlces today, Anthony Norris Groves (1795-1853) was, according to the writer of this book, one of the most influential men of the nineteenth century. He was what might be termed a spiritual pioneer, forging a path through unfamiliar territory in order that others might follow. One of those who followed him was George Müller, known to the world as one who in his lifetime cared for over ten thousand orphans without any appeal for human aid, instead trusting God alone to provide for the daily needs of this large enterprise.

In 1825 Groves wrote a booklet called *Christian Devotedness* in which he encouraged fellow believers and especially Christian workers to take literally Jesus' command not to lay up treasures on earth, but rather to give away their savings and possessions toward the spread of the gospel and to embark on a life of faith in God alone for the necessaries of life. Groves himself took this step of faith: he gave away his fortune, left his lucrative dental practice in England, and went to Baghdad to establish the first Protestant mission to Arabic-speaking Muslims. His going was not in connection with any church denomination or missionary society, as he sought to rely on God alone for needed finances. He later went to India also.

His approach to missions was to simplify the task of churches and missions by returning to the methods of Christ and His apostles, and to help indigenous converts form their own churches without dependence on foreign support. His ideas were considered radical at the time but later became widely accepted in evangelical circles.

Groves was a leading figure in the early days of what Robert Govett would later call the mightiest movement of the Spirit of God since Pentecost—a movement that became known simply as the Brethren. In this book G. H. Lang combines a study of the life and influence of Anthony Norris Groves with a survey of the original principles and practices of the Brethren movement.

www.ingramcontent.com/pod-product-compliance
Lightning Source LLC
Chambersburg PA
CBHW060824050426
42453CB00008B/581